36, 37, 38

27, 28, 29    13, 14

THE COLUMBUS CENTRE SERIES

# HUMAN DESTRUCTIVENESS

# THE COLUMBUS CENTRE SERIES

## STUDIES IN THE DYNAMICS OF PERSECUTION AND EXTERMINATION

*General Editor: Norman Cohn*

ANTHONY STORR
*Human Destructiveness*

HENRY V. DICKS
*Licensed Mass Murder*

DONALD KENRICK & GRATTAN PUXON
*The Destiny of Europe's Gypsies*

Forthcoming
LEON POLIAKOV
*The Aryan Myth*

# HUMAN
# DESTRUCTIVENESS

*By*

Anthony Storr

BASIC BOOKS, INC., *Publishers*

NEW YORK

152.4
S886h

1/3/75

© 1972 by Anthony Storr
Library of Congress Catalog Card Number: 72-76923
SBN: 465-03129-3
Printed in the United States of America
72  73  74  75  10  9  8  7  6  5  4  3  2  1

# Contents

Editorial Foreword     vii

1   The Nature of Human Aggression     9

2   Psychopathy     34

3   Sado-Masochism     48

4   The Ubiquity of Paranoia     80

References     116

Index     123

# EDITORIAL FOREWORD

Following a proposal originally advanced by the Hon. David Astor, a research centre was set up in the University of Sussex in 1966 to investigate how persecutions and exterminations come about; how the impulse to persecute or exterminate is generated, how it spreads, and under what conditions it is likely to express itself in action. The Centre was originally called the Centre for Research in Collective Psychopathology but later adopted the more neutral name of the Columbus Centre, after the Trust which finances it.

The Centre's work has now resulted in a series of books and monographs on subjects ranging from the roots of European nationalism and racism to the fate of the Gypsies as a minority, from the causes of the persecution of 'witches' to the causes of the exterminations carried out under the Third Reich, and from the biological to the psychological roots of the very urge to persecute or to exterminate.

From the beginning, the Centre's work was designed on a multi-disciplinary basis. The disciplines represented in the present series include history, sociology, anthropology, dynamic psychology and ethology. Moreover, while the research was being done and the books written, the various authors constantly exchanged ideas and information with one another. As a result while each book in the series belongs to a single discipline and is the work of a single author, who alone carries responsibility for it, the series as a whole is coloured by the experience of inter-disciplinary discussion and debate.

The enterprise was also designed on an international scale. Although this has been a British project in the sense that it was sponsored by a British university and that 95 per cent of its finance was also British, the people who did the research and wrote the books came from several countries. Indeed, one of them was a Frenchman who worked in Paris throughout, another a German who worked in Berlin. Everything possible was done to exclude national bias from a study which might all too easily have been distorted by it.

vii

The work was financed throughout by the Columbus Trust. It was originally made possible by massive donations to the Trust from the Hon. David Astor, the late Lord Sieff of Brimpton and Sir Marcus Sieff, and the Wolfson Foundation, promptly followed by further generous contributions from Mr Raymond Burton, the Rt Hon. Harold Lever, Mr I. J. Lyons, Mr Hyam Morrison, Mr Jack Morrison, Sir Harold Samuel, the American Jewish Committee, the J. M. Kaplan Fund, Inc., and the William Waldorf Astor Foundation. His Grace the Archbishop of Canterbury, Sir Leon Bagrit, Lord Evans of Hungerfall, and Messrs Myers & Company, also showed their goodwill to the enterprise by giving it financial assistance.

Since the Centre came into existence many people have devoted a great deal of time and energy to the various financial and advisory committees associated with it. They include the chairman of the Columbus Trust, the Rt. Hon. the Lord Butler of Saffron Walden; two successive Vice-Chancellors of the University of Sussex, Lord Fulton of Falmer and Professor Asa Briggs; the Hon. David Astor, Professor Max Beloff, Professor Sir Robert Birley, Professor Patrick Corbett, Professor Meyer Fortes, Dr Robert Gosling, Mr Ronald Grierson, Professor Marie Jahoda, Dr Martin James, Professor James Joll, the Rt Hon. Harold Lever, Professor Barry Supple, Dr John D. Sutherland, Professor Eric Trist, Professor A. T. M. Wilson, Mr Leonard Wolfson, and the Registrar and Secretary of the University, Mr A. E. Shields, who has acted as the secretary of the Centre's Management Committee. It is a pleasure to acknowledge the support and counsel they have so willingly given.

The series also owes a great deal to the devoted service of the late Miss Ursula Boehm, who was the administrative secretary to the Centre from its inception until her death in 1970.

NORMAN COHN

# THE NATURE OF HUMAN
# AGGRESSION

This monograph forms part of a research project designed
to investigate, and to give some tentative explanation
of, human destructiveness; more particularly, of that
form of human destructiveness which is directed towards the persecution and extermination of other
human beings. The contribution which any human
being, from whatever academic background, can make
is necessarily limited, but it is hoped that, by pooling
the combined experiences of persons with different
training and experience, some conclusions may emerge
which will be of value in understanding the phenomenon of destructiveness and hence point the way to
its ultimate control. In such a venture the contribution
of the practising psychotherapist is open to question.
Human destructiveness on a large scale is, obviously
enough, the problem with which we ought chiefly to
be concerned. We seek to understand and to obviate
the horrors of ideological war, of the concentration
camp, of racial violence. Such large themes must surely
be the province of the historian, the sociologist and
the political scientist. The psychotherapist, closeted all
day in his consulting room, is concerned only with the
emotional problems of distressed individuals. Moreover, his experience is almost entirely limited to a
highly selected class of individuals who might briefly
be described as Western-educated, sophisticated, intelligent, complex and prosperous. Are the deductions
which he makes from the study of such individuals

of any value in understanding such diverse phenomena as the Nazi concentration camp, the race riots of Detroit, the Armenian massacres, or the diverse causes of tension between sovereign states? It could well be argued that they are not.

Psychotherapists are much too apt to extrapolate from their study of a few neurotic individuals, to reduce the complex to the over-simple, and to assume that the forces which account for the behaviour of nations are the same as those which drive their patients. There is still comparatively little exchange between politicians and psychiatrists, although it is encouraging to note that Senator J. William Fulbright takes the psychiatric point of view seriously enough to write an introduction to Jerome D. Frank's recent book on psychological aspects of war and peace, *Sanity and Survival*.[1] Moreover, there is still such disagreement between psychologists, psychiatrists and psychoanalysts upon the nature of human aggressiveness that John Burton is justified in writing: "We are by no means certain that aggression is a prime motivation in animals or men, and even if we were, it would not necessarily follow that aggressiveness can be attributed to nation-states." Dr Burton, who is an expert in international affairs, argues that aggression is the result of fear, frustration, and deprivation; and believes that if this was realized, instead of the assumption being made that states were motivated by some 'inevitable aggressive urge', foreign policies would have to be considerably modified. "The seemingly aggressive policies of states would then be perceived, not as struggles for power for its own sake, but as a power-struggle designed to avoid the consequences of aggressiveness by others which has unjustifiably been assumed to exist."[2]

This is a powerful and interesting argument. The unjustified assumption of aggressiveness in others is a likely cause of international quarrels; and one which the psychiatrist will recognize as familiar. Man's tendency to project upon others his own unacknowledged hostility is a feature of human behaviour to which we shall often revert in what follows. Yet it is hard to believe that this kind of paranoid misapprehension is responsible for all warlike activities. Were the Viking raids of A.D. 800-1100 entirely the result of 'fear, frustration and deprivation'? It seems unlikely. Professor Brønsted, in his book on the subject, admits that some degree of over-population may have contributed to these violent predations; but he rates much higher the desire for wealth by gaining command of trade-routes, with the opportunities for piracy which such command afforded. Moreover, he recognizes that the emotional characteristics of the Vikings themselves were crucial. Although the Vikings may have been frustrated by their increasing numbers, and envious of the wealth of other nations, their psychology and Weltanschauung were equally important. "But in appraising these factors there is one which lies outside mercantile considerations, and that is the characteristic Nordic way of life. This was a compound of daring, adventurousness, and belligerence. The Vikings were possessed by a desire to excel in battle, by a thirst for glory and a scorn for death."[3]

In nuclear war, opportunities for heroism or the demonstration of virility may be minimal; but the desire to display these qualities is not confined to the Vikings, and must be taken into account when considering national aggressiveness.

Whatever political and social factors may be important in determining the behaviour of nations, it remains true that decisions are ultimately made by individuals, and that these individuals will be influenced both by the conception of human nature which is current at the time, and also by the way they themselves have learned to cope with their own natures. In this field the psychotherapist may have something to add to the wider perspectives of his historical, sociological, and economist colleagues; for his daily work is much concerned with how individuals control, or fail to control, violent impulses within themselves.

That this is the case may still be insufficiently appreciated by the general public. It is often supposed that psychotherapy, and more especially Freudian psychoanalysis, is chiefly preoccupied with the complex ramifications of the sexual impulse, which, thanks to Freud, we now recognize to have its origin in childhood in common with other instincts. No analyst would be inclined to deny the enormous importance of sexuality in the economy of the human psyche; but it is easy to demonstrate that, since the time of Freud's earliest formulations, psychoanalysts have become increasingly concerned with human aggression and hostility. This is particularly the case in England, where the conceptions of Melanie Klein have taken firmer root than in other parts of the world. The English, though unfriendly to strangers, are in general orderly, controlled and not much given to violence. It may be that a psychology which postulates that the beginning of our psychic existence is fraught with hatred and fear of retaliation has a particular appeal to the apparently urbane and disciplined English; but this I must leave to the sociologist to determine. What is undoubted is that, over the last thirty years or so, psychoanalysis has increasingly affirmed the importance of hostile and destructive impulses in understanding the psychology of the individual, whilst continuing to acknowledge the equally vital role of sexuality. This being so, it may seem surprising that there is no general agreement upon the subject. For, whilst psychologists agree that human aggression is ubiquitous, some maintain that it is invariably the product of frustration, and thus avoidable, whilst others aver that it is part of man's instinctive equipment, and thus inevitable.

At present there is a lively debate proceeding upon this controversial topic: a debate which is disfigured by the extreme and often 'aggressive' statements of some of the protagonists. Thus Ashley Montagu, an anthropologist working in America, goes so far as to state: "The notable thing about *human* behaviour is that it is learned. Everything a human being does as such he has had to learn from other human beings." And later he writes: "The fact is, that with the exception of the instinctoid reactions in infants to sudden withdrawals of support, and to sudden loud noises, the human being is entirely instinctless." He goes on to attack Konrad Lorenz and Robert Ardrey, who take the opposite point of view, in terms so intemperate that the psychiatrist is tempted to enquire what makes Mr Montagu himself quite so aggressive. His explanation of man's aggression and destructiveness is "the many false and contradictory values by which, in an over-crowded, highly competitive, threatening world, he so disoperatively attempts to live. It is not man's nature, but his nurture, in such a world, that requires our attention." Mr Montagu believes, on the basis of his knowledge of primitive man, that hostilities between groups of men seldom if ever "occurred before the development of agricultural-pastoral communities, not much more than 12,000 years ago".[4]

Yet other anthropologists paint a very different picture of primitive man. "Throughout most of human evolution man was adapted to ways of life radically different from those of today and there has been neither the time nor the control of breeding to change the biology of human aggression from what was adaptive in the past to what is adaptive now. Throughout most of human history, society has depended on young adult males to hunt, to fight and to maintain the social order with violence."[5] Moreover, in a recent book, Robert Bigelow argues not only that primitive man lived in small groups which were indeed perpetually hostile to one another, but that it was actually warfare which was responsible for the enormous evolutionary increase in the size of the human brain. Whether this is so or not, Mr Bigelow produces an impressive array of examples which tend to show that the earliest human groups were invariably hostile to one another just as are the few 'stone-age' peoples surviving today in the remoter valleys of New Guinea. He takes the wholly sensible view that "behavior as complex as human warfare is *both* innate *and* intelligent", and accuses

Ashley Montagu of "believing in the peacefulness of primitive men with a missionary zeal".[6] This opinion is shared by Konrad Lorenz who writes: "Indeed, the deep emotional disturbance so clearly apparent in many adversaries of ethological theory is far more intense than that ever elicited in one scientist by the errors of another, however stupid and however irritatingly presented they may be. Religious fervour like this is only aroused in men who sense the explosion of a long-cherished dogma. Ashley Montagu has formulated that dogma with all desirable clarity: man is devoid of instincts, all human behavior is learned."[7] Montagu accuses Lorenz and others of having revived the religious doctrine of original sin; but to assume that no innate or instinctive factors enter into human behaviour is surely to revive the pre-Darwinian point of view that man is a special creation, unrelated to any other animal, and quite unlike any of his primate cousins. The dispute as to whether man's aggression is partly innate or wholly learned has itself roused aggressive passions which are worth our attention, and to which we shall return when discussing why it is that men are apt to torture and kill other men for no apparent reason than that they hold different beliefs.

Of course, as with so many disputes, part of the trouble is semantic. The word 'aggression' is itself a notable culprit. The *Shorter Oxford English Dictionary* gives as its first definition of 'aggression': 'An unprovoked attack; the first attack in a quarrel; an assault.' Psychologists use the word in this sense; but they also use it in the antique or original sense of active movement towards. The first, now obsolete, definition of

15

the verb 'aggress' is simply given as 'to approach'. If we substitute other prefixes before the same root we have 'egress', 'regress', 'progress' and 'ingress': words which indicate movement outwards, backwards, forwards, and inwards respectively, without any further meaning or emotional overtones implied (although it is true that regression has acquired a special meaning in psychology). According to the same dictionary, it was in the eighteenth century that 'aggress' began to be used in the sense of beginning a quarrel. At present, some psychologists use the word aggression when referring to behaviour which is not necessarily hostile or the result of hate. The drive to master the environment, to wrest from it what is needed for survival, is, in the way these psychologists use the term, an 'aggressive drive'; an active striving towards, as opposed to passive waiting or withdrawal. Unfortunately, this usage has given rise to some confusion even amongst psychoanalysts, many of whom have remained ignorant of, or uninfluenced by, modern ethological thought. Thus, in his *Critical Dictionary of Psychoanalysis*, under the heading 'Aggression', Rycroft writes: "The almost universal tendency of analysts to equate aggression with hate, destructiveness, and sadism runs counter to both its etymology (*ad-gradior*: I move forwards) and to its traditional meaning of dynamism, self-assertiveness, expansiveness, drive."[8]

It might be thought that confusion could easily be avoided by inventing or appropriating some term to designate 'active striving towards', whilst reserving the word 'aggression' for 'unprovoked attack'. Unfortunately, this cannot easily be done; for, as in other

16

semantic dilemmas, the double usage indicates that there is an area of experience in which the two concepts *are* connected, and that to try to separate them might make confusion worse confounded. As Schilder puts it: "It is difficult to distinguish between activity, which is a general characteristic of life, and aggressiveness. . . . This activity in aggressiveness has a close relation to motor drives and to instincts in general. It doubtless has its foundation in the organic structure, and its variations are in close relation to the child's constitution. Organic processes may influence the general output of energy. The hyperkinetic child shows a great increase, not only in activity, but also in aggressiveness." In another passage, he writes "Man, as a carnivorous animal, must kill in order to live. . . . In his relation to plants and the inanimate world, man makes use of his strength. He has to destroy structures and use material without regard for their inner organization. A close relationship exists between such activities and aggressiveness towards animals and human beings. Thus, Freud has offered the theory that these 'instincts of the ego', which serve self-preservation, are identical with the destructive tendencies, and that they are primarily directed toward one's self and only secondarily towards the outer world."[9]

We can, indeed I think we must, accept Freud's idea that self-preservation and destructive or 'aggressive' tendencies are closely allied: but we need not accept his notion of a death instinct primarily directed against the self. I am entirely in agreement with Schilder, when in another paper, he writes: "It seems to me that the existence of a death impulse is questionable. . . . The striving toward the external world, toward grasping and mastery, seems to us so elemental that we cannot look upon it as a derivative of the impulses to self-annihilation.''[10]

Just as the hyperkinetic child shows an increase in aggressiveness *pari passu* with his increase in activity, the person whose aggressiveness is inhibited or repressed shows a decrease in activity. In severe depression, it can be shown that the sufferer is invariably suppressing or repressing intensely violent feelings, usually directed towards some person close to him in the immediate environment. Severely depressed people also show a diminution of initiative and motor activity which, in psychotic cases, may reach the point of almost complete immobilization. Children in whom aggression has been too severely punished often show a reluctance to initiate activity, an increase in fear of the aggression of other children, since they are not 'allowed' to stand up for themselves, and even a falling-off in school work, since they cannot 'attack' or master a subject properly. Most of us would like to rid ourselves of the destructive aspects of our aggression; but it is difficult to do so without impairing the necessary and positive aspects of the aggressive drive. The bathwater of hostility is all too likely to drain away with it the baby of initiative.

Nevertheless, there is a proper distinction to be made between aggression and hatred, to which we shall often revert. When a man goes hunting for food, or cuts down a tree to make himself a dwelling, he is actively striving towards gaining from the environment the food and shelter which he needs. It may be alleged, with reason, that he feels no hatred towards the animal he kills or the tree he sacrifices; yet he is making an unprovoked attack upon each. It is true that, if the animal eluded and exhausted him, or if the tree proved particularly resistant to his axe, the man might well come to 'hate' both, and to show undue violence to both, since frustration undoubtedly increases aggression, although it does not, in my view, cause it. The point at which aggression turns into hatred will be discussed later.

Even the exercise of aggression in warfare need not be accompanied by hatred; a fact which, in pre-nuclear days, may have partly accounted for warfare's continued popularity. This is not to deny that some wars have been undertaken for purely instrumental reasons; that is, to gain the increased food-supply and 'lebensraum' which the acquisition of territory may bring. But it is important to realize that there is, or rather was, an enjoyable aspect even to war. Indeed, the Greeks had a word for the 'spirit of battle', χάρμη, which, according to the learned Professor Onians, "is most naturally connected with χαίρω, χάρμα, χαρμονή and interpreted to mean in origin something like 'joy. . . . Boisacq (s.v.) connects both χαίρω and χάρμη with a conjectural Indo-European gher(e) expressing desire of various kinds including anger. χάρμη will be the 'battle-lust' or 'joy' that comes with free play of the warrior's energies, when like the war-horse he 'smelleth the battle afar off'. When 'warring becomes sweeter than returning home' and battle—to sweep over the field with instincts and energies free—is 'joy' indeed, the supreme realization of the pride of power."[11]

This 'joyful' aspect of aggression is, naturally enough, most sought after by those young adult males who, as Professor Washburn remarked, have been required by society to "hunt, to fight and to maintain the social order with violence"; and one of the problems faced by modern societies is to provide suitable outlets for the aggressive energies of young males who are still genetically programmed for such aggressive activities but who, in urban societies, have little legitimate opportunity for aggressive expression.

If we are to understand man's destructiveness, it is vital that we distinguish between aggression as 'active striving', the drive towards mastering the environment, which is both desirable and necessary for survival; and aggression as 'destructive hostility', which we generally deplore, and which seems to militate *against* survival, at least of the species, if not of the individual. Self-preservation and the preservation of the species demand that we actually strive toward obtaining food, space and the acquisition of a mate with whose co-operation we can reproduce ourselves. In the pursuit of what we need for survival and self-realization we are necessarily competitive, and thus 'aggressive'; but there is no obvious reason why we should be destructive, provided we can gain satisfaction for our basic needs. On account of various historical and emotional factors which I have discussed elsewhere, Freud came late to the recognition of aggression as a separate entity; and, when he finally did so, concluded that aggression towards the external world was a redirection of destructive energy which was primarily aimed at the self. This notion of the 'death instinct' has not been accepted by the majority of analysts, who rightly regard it as unbiological. If, however, we discard the concept of a 'death instinct' which I, for one, am happy to do, psychoanalysis and many of its derivatives fall into line with the other 'life sciences' in regarding man primarily from the biological point of view. As one writer puts it, psychoanalysis "regards the self as a psychobiological entity which is always striving for self-realization and self-fulfilment. In other words, it regards mankind as sharing with the animal and plant world the intrinsic drive to create and recreate its own nature."[12]

Animals, including man, are obviously bound to be in competition with one another, unless the resources of the environment are so profuse that there is easily available more than enough for all. Since competition for resources is inevitable, some method of ensuring that competing animals do not destroy each other in the struggle for existence is obviously required, or else the species would be in danger of exterminating itself. Nor is it only aggressive competition between individuals which constitutes a threat to the species. In the absence of checks and balances, the environment is habitually over-exploited, with the result that the terrain dries up as a source of supply.

In animals other than man, the preservation of the species is reconciled with the demands of the individual by the institution of conventions which ensure that the population does not so increase as to outstrip the resources of the terrain and that aggressive competition between individuals does not turn into destructive hostility. One such convention, which has been most extensively studied amongst birds, is the adoption of territory. As Wynne-Edwards put it: "The substitution of a parcel of ground as the object of competition in place of the actual food it contains, so that each individual or family unit has a separate holding of the resource to exploit, is the simplest and most direct kind of limiting convention it is possible to have. It is the commonest form of tenure in human agriculture. It provides an effective proximate buffer to limit the population-density at a safe level (which is obviously somewhere near the optimum though we can only guess in animals how nearly perfection is attained); and it results in spreading the population evenly over the habitat, without clumping them in groups as we find in many alternative types of dispersion." Man's power to use his brain to emancipate himself from conventions as well as to institute them has disposed of most of the checks upon the increase of his population (for example, prolonged lactation, child exposure, and disease). And the invention of agricultural tools and weapons has made it possible for him to escape from the natural checks which might have prevented him from exploiting the environment. For example, unrestricted over-fishing has led to permanent depletion of the stock of right-whales. Unregulated cultivation led to the creation of the so-called Dust Bowl in the mid-Western states of the U.S.A. Sophisticated methods of agriculture produced a rich reward for some years, but destroyed the thick, matted grass which covered the plains and protected the soil from dispersion by wind. Denuded of this protective covering, the top soil was simply lifted by the wind, making further agricultural use of the land impossible. Moreover, man, unlike other animals, is never satisfied; so that he will continue to compete for more and more possessions, territory, status, and wealth, even when his basic needs have been more than fully met. This characteristic, little commented on by psychoanalysts, is connected with the persistent sense of insecurity experienced by so many human beings which, like other specifically human attributes, seems to be the result of man's prolonged period of immaturity before adult status is attained. It is also connected with man's capacity for symbolization and idealization, which enables him to attribute to material possessions a psychological significance which does not belong to their intrinsic nature.

We mentioned above the institution of conventions. As Wynne-Edwards points out, for this to be effective, it is necessary that the contestants shall somehow or another be in communication with one another; or, in other words, form a society. If free enterprise and the principle of each individual for himself has to be sacrificed in some degree to the good of the community, then there has to be a community. As Wynne-Edwards puts it: "Any open contest must of course bring the rivals into some kind of association with one another; and we are going to find that, if the rewards sought are conventional rewards, then the association of contestants automatically constitutes a society. Putting the situation the other way round, a society can be defined for our purposes as *an organization capable of providing conventional competition*: this, at least, appears to be its original, most primitive function, which indeed survives more or less thinly veiled even in the civilized societies of man." After describing how male birds sing in order to be heard and recognized by their rivals, he goes on to write: "This two-faced property of brotherhood combined and tempered with rivalry is absolutely typical of social behaviour; both are essential to providing the setting in which conventional competition can develop."[13]

This illuminating concept throws light upon the conflict between the U.S.A. and the Soviet Union; a conflict which has extremely primitive roots. We can easily see why it so deeply engages the feelings of the protagonists on either side. For both are, in a sense, right. The American who defends individual initiative and free enterprise is defending the primeval right of the organism to seek its own self-realization and fulfilment. The Russian who puts society first is recognizing that we cannot and do not exist in isolation; and that if the human species is to survive, individualism must be limited, since society can be destroyed by unregulated competition. Animal societies which have not been too severely interfered with by man have solved this problem by adopting a variety of regulating conventions which are detailed in Wynne-Edwards's fascinating book. Human beings have not, to date, been so successful.

One convention which diminishes the likelihood of fatal conflict between animals of the same species is the substitution of threat and display for actual combat; together with the development of gestures of defeat or submission which have the effect of making the winner desist from further attack. Except in conditions of overcrowding or shortage of food-supply, it is rare for animals of the same species to kill each other, although some species may inflict some fairly fearsome looking injuries. Moreover, conventional rituals govern behaviour, not only between individuals belonging to the same group of animals, but between differing groups. "The relation between different groups of a population of wild primates will rarely degenerate into actual fighting, being mostly settled by means of long-range threatening or mere warning signals, if not by the discreet withdrawal of the smaller party. . . . From the many recent field studies it has become evident that nonhuman primates under natural conditions and regardless of differences in their social systems, generally lead peaceful lives and are certainly not nearly as aggressive and easily provoked creatures as used to be assumed from their behaviour under crowded conditions of captivity."[14]

Even competition for mates does not usually occasion destructiveness; for, although battles between males in the breeding season are common in many species, males who are defeated and do not acquire a mate merely remain as surplus members of the group without, as far as is known, being more destructive than their successful peers, at least in the sense of killing.

There is an exception to the general rule that aggressive competition between members of the same species is seldom lethal. This is to be found in creatures which form clans or colonies in which individual members recognize one another by smell. Social insects such as bees, termites and ants will destroy any member of another colony which strays into their midst; and so will rats and other rodents. The biological reason for this is obscure; for it is hard to see what adaptive purpose is served by the development of intense hostility between clan and clan, or colony and colony. It may be that if we could understand, in evolutionary terms, how this intergroup hostility in insects and rodents came about, we should better be able to understand our own hostility to other members of the human species. Smell certainly plays a part in some of the irrational distaste which human beings display towards other humans of a different colour or race. Anatomists have found considerable differences in human skin which "substantiate the classifications of physical anthropologists". One of these differences is in the number and chemical characteristics of the apocrine glands, which are responsible for a secretion giving a pungent smell. A Japanese anatomist visiting Europe found that Europeans smelt "strong, rancid, sweetish, sometimes bitter"; and negroes are often reported by those who are not negroes to smell musky. Carleton Coon also points out that human beings vary racially to an unusual degree. "In visible, external, mostly heritable characteristics, human beings vary more from place to place and race to race than any other mammalian species, except those that men have altered by domesticating them, most notably dogs."[15]

Since a great deal of human violence and cruelty occurs between individuals who are indistinguishable by smell, race, or other physical features, these differences cannot be adduced as explaining all human violence; but such factors are certainly contributory to some, and should not be neglected when considering the tensions between races which cause so much contemporary alarm.

If, therefore, we consider man as a primate, more advanced than, but still in line with, his animal cousins, it is really very odd that he is so destructive and so cruel to his own species. Animals have largely solved the problem of reconciling the needs of the individual with the preservation of the group; and by ritualizing aggression, have obviated destructiveness, whilst preserving dynamism. But men not only destroy each other in vast quantities; they are also cruel to each other. Unlike other animals, they are not content to let a defeated rival quit the fray without inflicting further injury. Torture, mutilation and other barbarities have been practised by men upon men since human history began; and many torturers have relished this exercise of arbitrary power. In a recent book, Claire and W. M. S. Russell attempted to show that human violence was invariably the result of the same stresses which produce violence within animal groups. Food shortage, overcrowding, confinement, and an imbalance of the sexes will all produce stress and subsequent violence in animal communities. We now know that Solly Zuckerman's famous study of the baboons on Monkey Hill in the London Zoo should not have been entitled *The Social Life of Monkeys and Apes*[16] but rather 'The Abnormal Social Life of Baboons under Stress of Confinement'. Moreover, the slaughter which Zuckerman described was the result, not only of confinement, but of a gross relative shortage of females.

The Russells believe that "violence is not the result of an innate propensity to aggression irrespective of conditions, but a response to stress in societies". They suggest that "violence is part of a complex of responses evolved to achieve drastic reduction of a population that is in danger of outgrowing its resources".[17] Both these statements contain a measure of truth; but the Russells overstate their case, especially when they seek to prove that early wars were invariably due to over-population. Statistics relating to remote periods of history can be no more than guesswork. I have no doubt that overcrowding produces violence in men as it does in monkeys; and that the prevalence of violence in the city streets of America and elsewhere is in part the result of stress from this cause. Nor do I dispute that war may be a regulating device for reducing population. If ever the hydrogen bomb is used in war, I think the most likely antecedent cause for its use will be the terrifyingly rapid increase in world population. But if man has no 'innate propensity to aggression' he must be grossly over-sensitive to stress. For perfectly normal men enjoy the exercise of aggression in the sense of the 'joy of battle' referred to earlier. Moreover, it is not at all difficult to persuade normal men to inflict pain, or to come to enjoy the practice of torture. No doubt, as the Russells allege, mass-murderers and parents who batter their babies (to give two examples of violent individuals) have experienced more than their share of neglect and violence themselves in their own early years. We do not doubt that the propensity to violence is much accentuated by the ill-effects of an unhappy childhood. But individuals who have not apparently been subjected to much stress, and who show no obvious sign of psychiatric abnormality, can be both violent and cruel; and, even if their behaviour could ultimately be shown to be the result of stress, then it must be a stress which is pretty well universal. As I hope to show later in my argument, the idea of a universal stress is by no means silly, for man is particularly vulnerable as a species to the effects of his early rearing; and an infancy and childhood without stress is almost inconceivable. But this is an argument based upon man's differences from other species of primate, not upon the idea that if only we all had ideal backgrounds we should have no propensity to violence.

Dr Jerome Frank, in his book *Sanity and Survival* to which we have already made reference, summarizes the now famous experiments of S. Milgram, who devised a situation in which normal American students believed that they were studying the effect of punishment upon learning. To this end they were required to administer electric shocks to a fellow subject each time he made a mistake in a simple learning task. Moreover, they were required to increase the severity of the shock after each mistake. The interesting and alarming finding was that these normal students would continue to give what they genuinely believed to be painful, or even potentially lethal, shocks to their fellows, in spite of warnings marked on the apparatus, simply because they were urged to by the experimenter.[18,19]

In other words, the human tendency to obey authority was much stronger than the equally human tendency to compassion. It is easy to see how much suffering can be inflicted by one sadistic person who attains a position of authority, especially if that authority is backed by the panoply of State or Church. There is no need to assume that all the torturers of the Inquisition were sadists. They were simply doing what they were told, in the sure belief that the Holy Office knew best and could not be wrong. In a later historical context, many Nazi 'war criminals' invoked the excuse of obedience to authority as mitigating their cruel and destructive behaviour: and similar pleas will no doubt be advanced by those American soldiers who have been accused of atrocities in Vietnam.

The human tendency to obey authority is probably connected with the fact that obedience is biologically adaptive for animals who live in groups. Most primates form dominance hierarchies in which the group is controlled either by a single, powerful overlord, or else by an oligarchy of the strongest males. These dominant individuals have the first right to food and to mate with females. They also form the centre of attention of the whole group, who move when they move, rest when they rest, and so on. In return for these privileges, the group may expect that these dominant individuals will protect them from predators; that it will gain from the experience of the older males; and that fighting within the group itself will be reduced to a minimum, since the dominant individuals will intervene to stop it. This arrangement is particularly noticeable in free-ranging primates like savannah baboons which traverse wide open areas with very little cover. In terrain of this kind, a closely-knit social structure based upon a rather tyrannical type of dominance is essential if the group is to be rapidly moved as a unit.[20]

An equivalent arrangement is to be found in human armies. Obedience to superiors is essential, not only because soldiers are required to carry out dangerous and distasteful duties from which they might normally recoil, but because it is often necessary to move large bodies of men as one unit. I do not think it is fanciful to assume that the human tendency to obey authority without enough question is a biologically rooted trait which was originally adaptive because it favoured the survival of the small tribal group which constituted the social unit of primitive man. Obedience is still adaptive in human society. One has only to think of the chaos which would ensue if most individuals did not, without thinking, obey the orders of policemen, or even of much less formidable individuals who happen to be given temporary authority like ushers in concert halls or at mass meetings. The most remarkable thing about human crowds is their sheeplike tendency to follow a leader, not the fact that they occasionally get out-of-hand.

We have disputed the Russells' notion that human violence and cruelty is necessarily the result of stress within society although acknowledging that stresses of the kind they catalogue are extremely important, both in animals and also in human societies. Is it instead to be explained by our in-built tendency to obey, which can so easily be exploited by a sadistic individual who happens to have gained power in the human hierarchy? Again, I believe that this explanation, although an important part of the truth, is no more than this. In order to understand human cruelty, it is of the utmost importance that we shall compare human behaviour with that of other animals, especially primates; for they are closest to us in the evolutionary scale. But this comparison will, I believe, lead us to link man's cruelty with those characteristics which are

31

peculiar to him, and which distinguish him from other animals. It is at this point that the contribution of the psychotherapist to the problem becomes relevant.

Although psychotherapists chiefly see individuals whom I have already characterized as highly selected, it is also true to say that they see a wide range of individuals with problems relating to the control and disposal of aggressive impulses, especially if they practise general psychiatry as well as psychotherapy. Some of these individuals are as near 'normal' as makes no difference. Indeed, their only abnormality may be to think that they are sufficiently abnormal to warrant consulting a psychiatrist. Certain kinds of upbringing predispose children to believe that desires and emotions which can be found in everybody are their own peculiar deviation. Other individuals may display a quite exceptional hostility and irritability in response to stimuli which most people would consider minimal. Still others may have so repressed their hostility that they have inhibited all the positive aspects of their aggression as well, with the result that their independence and initiative have been crippled. The study of these obviously unusual individuals can throw light upon 'normal' hostility and destructiveness, in exactly the same way that the study of disease in a bodily organ can throw light upon normal function. However, not all psychiatrically abnormal individuals are equally valuable for this purpose. Indeed, the very individuals whom the general public recognizes or thinks of as being most aggressive are perhaps the least illuminating. I shall argue that it is not the psychopaths nor the sadists whose emotional difficulties reveal most about 'normal' hostility, but those persons whom we label paranoid. In order to present this argument, however, it is necessary to discuss both psychopathy and sado-masochism, and the next part of this essay will be devoted to these subjects.

# PSYCHOPATHY

The diagnosis, or designation, 'psychopath' seems to have come into being because certain individuals showing abnormal or anti-social behaviour did not fit in to the conventional categories of neurosis or psychosis familiar to psychiatrists. It is partly because the term originated in this negative way that it is so unsatisfactory. The various categories of neurosis are based partly upon our observation of a patient's behaviour, but much more upon what he himself reports of his own mental experience, that is, his 'symptoms'. Only the patient himself can know whether he suffers from a compulsive thought, a phobia, or any but the more extreme varieties of anxiety and tension, since these are experiences which go on 'inside his own head' and produce but little external sign of their presence. In general, it is true to say that it is what neurotics complain of within their own subjective experience, rather than their behaviour or any appearance of illness, which leads to their consulting a psychiatrist. (There may be some exceptions to this general rule in the case of hysterics with amnesia or with gross conversion symptoms such as paralysis, deafness, or blindness.)

Psychotics, on the other hand, most often come to the attention of the psychiatrist through the complaints of others. The schizophrenic generally keeps his delusional system to himself. It is only when he has shown abnormal behaviour towards other people that an investigation of his subjective experience is instituted; and it may be very difficult to persuade him to reveal himself, since he generally believes that it is not he but others who are in the wrong. The manic patient, typically, feels himself to be unusually well; and although he may be causing chaos, shows little appreciation that there is anything wrong with him. Psychotic depressives are genuinely convinced that they are hopeless cases for whom nothing can be done, or attribute their state to an incurable physical disease. It is their relatives who instigate their treatment, not themselves.

Although there are a good many exceptions, it may be said with an approximation to truth that psychotics show disturbed behaviour without insight into their abnormal state of mind; and that neurotics show little disturbance of behaviour, but considerable insight. In the case of psychotics, clinical examination soon reveals the existence of mental abnormality which accounts for their unusual behaviour. In the case of neurotics, examination reveals the existence of controls, displacements and defences which inhibit behaviour, so that the neurotic expresses less of his wishes, instincts and impulses than the normal person.

The persons who have come to be labelled psychopathic fit into neither of these categories. In common with psychotics, they show disturbed or anti-social behaviour; and it is their relatives, or their victims, not they themselves, who complain. But examination of their mental state does not as a rule reveal the existence of delusional beliefs which account for their behaviour. Unlike neurotics, they show very little inhibition of impulse; and examination does not reveal the existence of defences and controls, but their absence. In other words, psychopaths are neither mad nor neurotic in the ordinary sense of these terms; but are clearly mentally abnormal in that they do not, or cannot, conform to the standards to which most people in the society adhere.

The term psychopath has been applied to a variety of unusual people, including some, like T. E. Lawrence, who have remarkable achievements to their credit. The chronically inadequate and dependent are also often labelled psychopathic, as are the sexually perverted, the schizoid, the alcoholic, the drug addicts and the tramps. In other words, the term has been used to designate so wide a variety of unusual human beings that it has become almost meaningless except as a word indicating disapproval or lack of comprehension. Nevertheless, there is still one category of person to whom the label can still be usefully applied, since there is a measure of agreement as to their most outstanding characteristics. It is also this category of psychopath which is most relevant to the theme of this essay.

'Aggressive psychopaths' are so named because their most outstanding characteristic is their use of violence to obtain their ends. In Western society, more especially in the upper and middle classes of society, the use of violence is severely discouraged; and liberally minded parents, who have learned to tolerate their young children's sexual interest and experimentation, are often deeply shocked by violent behaviour. Amongst the working classes physical violence is less subject to moral disapproval, more especially because it is the habitual method of punishment amongst the uneducated; but, even so, most children learn not to use violence as a direct means of getting what they want, although they may use it in response to frustration or threat. Aggressive psychopaths, however, have never learned to control their violent impulses, nor developed the kind of conscience which might deter them from using violence in order to take what they want if their wants are obstructed.

The reasons for this are various and complex. First, the development of a normal conscience seems to be chiefly the result of the wish to preserve love rather than the fear of punishment. That is, a child who has been loved by its parents will gradually make their moral standards its own, and learn to conform to what they expect, because he wishes to keep the parents' love and fears its withdrawal. Punishment, especially physical punishment, has the effect of increasing resentment and hostility; and, although severe punishment may cause a child to suppress the expression of hostility for fear of reprisal, it is not so effective a creator of conscience as the fear of the withdrawal of love. Conscience continues to operate even when there is no immediate expectation of punishment for aggressive behaviour; whereas children who have not developed an internal regulator of behaviour only restrain their aggressive impulses if there is an obvious threat of immediate punishment. Reviewing the literature on this subject, Berkowitz remarks: "There is a remarkable consistency to these findings. The studies reviewed here agree in noting that punitive parental disciplinary methods (such as physical punishment and depriving children of privileges) tend to be associated with a high level of aggression and other forms of anti-social behaviour by the children. Love-orientated disciplinary methods, on the other hand, evidently facilitate the development of conscience and internalized restraints against socially disapproved behaviour. Praising the child when he complies with parental standards and reasoning with him when he does not apparently are among the most effective of these love-orientated techniques."[21]

It is obvious that if the threat of the withdrawal of love is to operate as an effective restraint, there must have been some love between parent and child present in the first place. A child cannot respond to the withdrawal of something he has never had. It is not surprising, therefore, to discover that a high proportion of psychopaths are the product of broken homes, loveless homes, or impersonal institutions.

If a child does not receive love from parents during its early years, it will not incorporate their standards and develop a normal conscience. In addition to a lack of restraint of the aggressive impulses which are common to all children, the loveless child will develop an actual increase in the intensity of these impulses. For it seems that human beings have a basic need of love, and react to love's absence with resentment, even though they may appear not to know what they are missing. Although we talk of children being loveless, we must remember that every baby has had a mother, and is likely to have had some experience of being cuddled, caressed and cared for, however ephemerally. Babies who have no such experience at all are unlikely to survive. The psychopath, therefore, is suffering not only from an inadequacy of control of his hostility, but also from an increase in the intensity of what should be controlled. In an earlier piece of writing on the same subject, I compared the psychopath with the Miller of Dee. "I care for nobody, no not I; since nobody cares for me." It would probably be truer to say that many psychopaths hate everybody, because they have been deprived of the love to which human beings appear to feel that they are naturally entitled. As one prisoner told Tony Parker: "I hate this place, I hate the screws, I hate eating the food they give me, and wearing the clothes they tell me I have to put on. I hate everybody, that's the fact of it; and most of all I hate myself. Hatred, violence, I'm full of it, I think if I had the chance I'd destroy the whole world."[22]

One factor, therefore, in the production of aggressive psychopaths is the absence of loving care from parents in early childhood. Another is an apparent failure of the nervous system to mature normally. In about one-third of aggressive psychopaths electro-encephalography reveals abnormalities of the electrical activity of the brain. These abnormalities are generally of a type suggesting the persistence into adult life of rhythms characteristic of childhood. This finding is not surprising, since lack of control over immediate impulse is typical of childhood, and we do not expect a young child to be able to exercise much self-discipline. In at least some instances, the lack of control shown by psychopaths is as little their 'fault' as the temper tantrums of a two-year-old. Moreover, this cerebral abnormality may also show itself in relation to chemical changes. Some persons with electro-encephalographic abnormalities are unusually susceptible to minor changes in blood chemistry. Thus, a small amount of alcohol, which would hardly affect a normal person, may render these people entirely incapable of control; and so may a reduction in blood sugar. We are all familiar with the fact that irritability tends to increase *pari passu* with the time interval since our last meal. Examiners are apt to be more lenient after lunch than before it; and many people feel the need of a restorative drink around six o'clock when their blood sugar is probably at its lowest since lunch-time, unless they indulge themselves in tea and its accompaniments. Both small children and psychopaths with abnormal electro-encephalograms are easily affected by a low blood sugar.

In addition to the chemical and electro-encephalographic factors, active research is now going on into genetic factors. A small proportion of violent criminals shows an abnormality of the sex chromosomes; and although it is not yet possible to assess how important this factor is, or exactly how it may be related to psychopathic abnormality, yet there is little doubt of its importance in some cases.

Yet another factor is a probably constitutional difference between people with respect to how easily they are conditioned. Eysenck, in his book *Crime and Personality*, alleges that extraverts are much less easily conditioned than introverts, and that the majority of delinquents and criminals belong to the extraverted type. Eysenck, leaning heavily upon the work of Lange, believes that studies of identical twins have demonstrated that "Criminality is obviously a continuous trait of the same kind as intelligence, or height, or weight,"[23] and that the inherited element is the most important predisposing factor. He recommends the use of drugs and the method of conditioning known as 'behaviour therapy' in attempting to induce socially acceptable responses and discourage anti-social behaviour in criminals; but whether or not such methods would be successful we have no means of telling since they have not yet been tried. To the psychotherapist's way of thinking, conditioning methods alone, without the attempt to integrate the criminal into a community, make him feel valued as a person, or improve his interpersonal relationships, are likely to be short-lived in their effects. A great many psychopathic people are like the Irishman referred to above in the quotation from Tony Parker's book *The Frying-Pan*, hating everybody, and most of all hating themselves. That same interview ends with the man saying: "I'd sooner be anyone else there was than me." This man had indeed been treated for alcoholism with aversion therapy, one of the original and best-tried methods of behaviour therapy advocated by Eysenck; but without result. The emotional needs of such people may be impossible to meet; but re-conditioning them without any attempt to do so is clearly inadequate.

Whatever the causes of their abnormality (and, as with most psychiatric problems, the causes are multiple), aggressive psychopaths show a generalized lack of inhibitory control over both aggressive and other impulses. The same man who becomes violent on little provocation is likely to drive his car dangerously and to commit sexual offences. He will also show a lack of foresight and a disregard for the immediate consequences of his actions which both demonstrates the futility of 'deterrence' by threatened punishment, and also reveals another feature of his likeness to children, whom we do not expect to be able to look far ahead.

The same lack of relationship with other human beings which has precluded the development of a normal conscience accounts for the failure of the psychopath to identify himself with other human beings or to care what they suffer. We expect that a small child will regard those who care for him exclusively from a 'selfish' point of view. The younger the child, the more will he think of other people merely as instruments to provide for his own needs, and the less will he consider them as having needs of their own. Indeed, the infant lives in so solipsistic a world that he cannot at first distinguish the mother as a separate entity or himself as a finite being. The appreciation of other human beings as being worthy of as much consideration as himself comes late in childhood emotional development. Moreover, this appreciation is dependent upon the ties of love. 'Normal' people, who have experienced love in childhood, learn to care for those who love them reciprocally; and to appreciate that parents and siblings have a need for love in return. They gradually learn, therefore, not to 'hurt other people's feelings', to give as well as to take; and find that consideration of others is worthwhile, since it leads to obtaining more love and hence more self-esteem. Where love is absent, or where some constitutional abnormality has rendered the individual incapable of responding to love (for not all psychopaths appear to come from loveless homes), the conditions for learning to appreciate the needs and separate existence of others have simply not been present. It is not surprising, therefore, that the psychopath entirely disregards the rights of other people, values them only in so far as they satisfy his own immediate needs, and is indifferent to their pain and suffering if his own needs are being obstructed.

This is not quite so far from 'normal' as might at first appear. Even the most loving human being is capable of only a limited range of sympathies. It is difficult to make the imaginative effort to care deeply for human beings who belong outside the limited circle of relatives and friends. We may be shocked by newspaper accounts of famine in India, earthquakes in Peru, or tidal waves in Japan; but it is unlikely that these disasters will touch our hearts in the same way as the bereavement of a friend, or the death of one of our own loved ones. Psychopaths tend to regard even those in their immediate environment with the same indifference as a European shows to an unknown peasant in China. It is therefore not surprising that he shows little remorse for violence or other violation of the rights of others, since it is only a very few people, if any, who 'mean anything' to him.

The same underlying lack of relation accounts for the psychopath's disregard of truth. If other people are 'fair game', and there are no ties of identification with them, there is no reason to tell them the truth, any more than there is to any enemy in war-time. Indeed much psychopathic conduct is easy to understand if it is realized that psychopaths live in a world which they assume to be either completely indifferent to their welfare, or else actively hostile to it. If lying is more likely than the truth to gain their ends, then psychopaths will lie with no more conscience than a captured soldier will lie to his captors. In addition, many aggressive psychopaths tell lies which show that they have little appreciation of the difference between fact and phantasy; another characteristic they share with children. Many invent fantastic stories about themselves, designed to convince both themselves and others of their own importance, and obtain money or other advantages by these 'false pretences'. Such lying is indeed an aggressive weapon, but it is perhaps too far removed from our theme of violence and cruelty to warrant further consideration here.

What light does a study of psychopathic people throw upon our main theme, of human cruelty and destructiveness in general? First, there can be no doubt that such a study does indicate the importance of frustration in increasing a tendency to cruelty and violence, although not everyone would agree that it is the only cause of such a tendency. People who, like many psychopaths, have been deprived of affection or who have never had any, are resentful on this account, and are predisposed to react with violence to additional frustrations. Second, an upbringing in which love is absent and physical punishment frequent will further predispose the child so reared to use violence itself in later life. Third, such an upbringing prevents the formation of a normal conscience. Conscience is dependent upon the introjection of parental standards of consideration for others; and this introjection only appears to take place satisfactorily where deprivation of love (parental disapproval) rather than punishment is the chief operative factor in controlling the child's behaviour. Fourth, control over violent impulses is dependent not only upon possessing a normal conscience, but upon organic, physical factors many of which are as yet ill-understood. At least some violent characters show genetic abnormalities. Others show what appears to be a failure of development of the nervous system, as manifested by the persistence of immature electrical rhythms in the electro-encephalogram. This immaturity is a rather generalized trait in psychopaths which manifests itself in many areas of behaviour in addition to that of violent behaviour which is our especial concern.

The study of psychopaths, therefore, appears to go some way towards confirming the hypothesis that if human beings were not frustrated or genetically or physiologically abnormal, there would be no reason for them to be violent or aggressive.

Against this is the fact that not all psychopaths show genetic, physiological, or electro-encephalographic abnormalities; and not all come from loveless homes. Of course, our methods of study are not far advanced; and it may yet be possible to demonstrate physical abnormalities of some kind in all psychopaths. Yet there must remain a core of doubt that such explanations are insufficient.

As we have said, the most striking feature of psychopathic behaviour is the lack of control over impulse, whether this be violent or not. In the case of psychopaths who have come from loveless homes, this tendency toward violence is easy to explain on the frustration-aggression hypothesis. But what about the psychopaths who do not come from unloving homes? Their behaviour may be explained by a physiological lack; but the fact that they have so much aggression to control is not. Not all psychopaths are frustrated, loveless children; or rather, they are not more frustrated and loveless than the average child, so far as one can make out. What the study of psychopaths has to teach us is chiefly about the development of controlling mechanism over impulse in human beings. It tells us little about why such control should be so essential. Even normal human beings have to learn to moderate their violence as they grow up. The origin of human violence and cruelty is less illuminated by the study of psychopaths than at first appears.

Moreover, there is a distinction to be made between deliberate cruelty and casual violence. Most psychopathic criminals show the latter rather than the former. They may not hesitate to crack the skull of a night-watchman who tries to obstruct a robbery, or to attack an innocent old woman in the process of taking her handbag. They may murder a woman who has aroused sexual desire in them and then frustrated it. But the greater part of psychopathic violence is unpremeditated, casual, and provoked by some obviously frustrating cause in the immediate environment. It is indifference to the effect of violence upon others which is chiefly characteristic of psychopaths, not pleasure in its use. This indifference certainly argues a defect in relating to others; but it is a defect of emotional development, not necessarily an absolute or quantitative difference. From what we know of the attitude of small children to other persons, it is natural enough

46

to react with immediate violence to the obstruction of one's wants; and it is only a long period of training which brings this violence under control. If small babies possessed the physical strength and co-ordination of adolescents we should indeed live in a destructive world. Psychoanalysts who specialize in the study of children have no doubt as to the extreme aggressiveness of the frustrated infant. "The baby's typical response, say to acute hunger, is a reaction in which the whole body is involved; screaming, twitching, twisting, kicking, convulsive breathing, evacuations—all evident signs of overwhelming anxiety. Analytic evidence shows without any doubt that this reaction to the accumulated tension represents and is felt to be an *aggressive* discharge, as we should in any case imagine."[24] Whether or not it is inevitable that infants should be frustrated will be discussed at a later point in this essay. The point to be emphasized here is that very many human beings react with violent rage early in life, and that some, notably aggressive psychopaths, never, or only late in life, succeed in learning to control this violence.

Bradford College Library
Bradford, Massachusetts 01830

# SADO-MASOCHISM

I suggested above that most psychopathic violence was casual rather than deliberate: the violence which accompanies robbery is not generally cruelty indulged in for its own sake. But what about the so-called sadists? Sadistic murderers, like Ian Brady, and Neville Heath, are fortunately rare; but they do as a rule conform to the diagnostic category of 'psychopath' since they exhibit, in addition to their sadism, the traits of personality and defects of character which we have outlined above. But sadism is itself no essential part of psychopathy, and indeed exists in its absence, at least in phantasy, in many persons who are not psychopathic at all. The difference between the sadistic psychopath and persons with sado-masochistic inclinations who are not psychopaths is that the former are apt to enact their phantasies, whereas the latter are not—another illustration of the fact that lack of control over impulse is one of the chief features of psychopathy. That sado-masochism has a wide appeal, at least in Western culture, is obvious to anyone who looks with a critical eye at contemporary cinema, theatre and fiction. Nor is this a contemporary phenomenon only, although there is, at the time of writing, a new freedom of expression allowed to what used to be concealed. A study of Victorian children's literature, for example, reveals a barbarism only to be surpassed by modern 'horror comics'. Jack Harkaway, a best-selling hero of the last thirty years of the Victorian period, has adventures in which a man is gradually eaten alive, and a

girl tortured with red-hot stones. Torture is an openly
revealed theme of W. S. Gilbert's *The Mikado* and *The
Yeomen of the Guard*. Many of the short stories of Conan
Doyle have sado-masochistic themes. Indeed, it could
be argued that the latter part of the Victorian era was
even more notable than our own in this preoccupation
with sado-masochism. As Steven Marcus points out,
there was an efflorescence of sado-masochistic literature
at this time especially concerned with flagellation, and
this literature continues to be produced today, as a
rapid glance at any pornographic bookshop will reveal.
Sado-masochistic acts of an extreme kind may be
carried out under special circumstance by 'normal'
people, as in the concentration camps; or by psychopathic people in ordinary circumstance. But sado-
masochistic phantasies are entertained by all kinds of
perfectly respectable people who would never act upon
their phantasies, and who are often deeply distressed
by them. A compulsive interest in flagellation, or in
'bondage', is often a horrifying preoccupation to a
respectable member of one of the learned professions;
but, as every practising analyst will recognize, it is an
extremely common phenomenon.

It may be true, as Marcus suggests, that sado-
masochistic preoccupations are compensatory phenomena, at any rate to some extent. "If pornography in
general amounted to a reversal of Victorian moral
ideals, then the literature of flagellation represented a
reversal of Victorian ideal personal standards for men.
The striking features of this literature are its childish-
ness, extreme incoherence, absence of focus, confusion
of sexual identity, and impulse toward play-acting or

role-playing. These qualities stand in marked contrast to the Victorian ideals of manliness, solidity, certitude of self, straightforwardness, sincerity and singleness of being."[25]

But if sado-masochistic interests were wholly phenomena of compensation, we should expect that a decline in such interests would have taken place during the last hundred years, *pari passu* with the declining emphasis upon Victorian ideals of masculinity and the general increase in 'permissiveness' so characteristic of our era. No such decline appears to have occurred. In Kinsey's investigations, 22 per cent of males admitted some erotic response to sado-masochistic stories. If, to this figure, we add the large number of males who are erotically aroused by fetish objects which suggest sado-masochistic relationships (tight clothing, high heels, boots, etc.) we are bound to conclude that a very high proportion of the male population has at least some interest in sado-masochism. Females show a much less marked interest in psychosexual stimuli of all kinds, and appear to be much less easily conditioned sexually than males. "We have, then, thirty-three bodies of data which agree in showing that the male is conditioned by sexual experience more frequently than the female. The male more often shares, vicariously, the sexual experiences of other persons, he more frequently responds sympathetically when he observes other individuals engaged in sexual activities, he may develop stronger preferences for particular types of sexual activity, and he may react to a great variety of objects which have been associated with his sexual activities. The data indicate that in all of these respects, fewer of the females have their sexual behaviour affected by such psychologic factors."[26]

Kinsey notes this male-female difference, but gives only a tentative explanation for it, since research data are lacking. At the time he was writing, the most likely difference appeared to be in the biochemistry of the cerebral cortex. Investigation of children's behaviour in groups, however, has demonstrated that there is a considerable difference between the sexes in the amount of aggressive behaviour displayed from a very early age. It seems likely, therefore, that the greater male predilection for sado-masochism (and possible other sexual deviations) may be related to his greater innate aggressiveness.

Whether or not this is so, there can be little doubt of the very widespread interest in sado-masochistic literature shown by males in Western culture. Can a study of this phenomenon throw any light on our main theme, the peculiar nature of human destructiveness and hostility? On the face of it, it might appear highly likely. For, as we pointed out above, one of the specifically human aspects of aggressive rivalry is the tendency not to be content with a ritual victory, but to pursue the defeated rival and inflict further pain and humiliation upon him. Animals other than man may be assumed to be free of sado-masochistic inclinations, since none appear to gain pleasure from inflicting pain upon another. But man, with his imagination, his power of symbolization, and his perpetual readiness for sexual activity, is able to gain pleasure in all kinds of indirect ways which are foreign to less-developed species. Is human cruelty really a sexual phenomenon?

In order to determine this, some discussion of the relation between aggression, dominance and sexuality must now be undertaken.

At an earlier point in this essay, when discussing human readiness to obey authority, I referred to the fact that most primates form hierarchies based upon dominance, and pointed out some of the advantages to be derived from such an arrangement. The structure of an army was adduced as one example of a dominance structure amongst human beings; but this might be regarded as a special case. Is such a structure present amongst human beings who are not organized in a military fashion, but living a normal social life? I believe that there is, and that what we usually refer to as 'status' in humans is closely equivalent to dominance in other primates. Roger Brown, in his book *Social Psychology* has written: "The dominance order found in many animal societies resembles a human status order in that it is also composed of inequalities of privilege and power. Dominance is like status also in its dependence upon individual differences and especially in its dependence upon age and sex. In dominance orders the male usually outranks the female and the mature animal the immature. This is also the usual way with human status orders. The determinants of animal dominance beyond sex and age seem to be strength, aggressiveness, weaponry, fearsomeness of appearance, and ability to bluff. These things are not irrelevant to human status."[27] Nor are they irrelevant to the study of sado-masochism. Some time during the nineteen-fifties, Professor Maslow, now at Brandeis University, and Mrs Claire Russell, already referred to above, independently decided that much apparent sexual behaviour, both in man and other primates, was not what it appeared to be, but was concerned much more with aggression, status, dominance, and related concepts than with sensual pleasure or with sexual satisfaction. Both Professor Maslow and Mrs Russell refer to the behaviour they are describing as 'pseudo-sex'.[28]

One of the remarkable features of behaviour which has been repeatedly observed in different species of primates is that behaviour patterns which are clearly sexual in their original intention are not used for sexual purposes, but to indicate or to establish dominance relationships. This is true of both male and female behaviour. In most monkeys and apes it is females who initiate sexual activity. This they do by *presenting*: that is, by approaching a male, turning the hind-quarters towards him, and, at the same time, looking backwards over the shoulder towards him. In many species, this invitation is underlined by the fact that when in heat, the whole perineal area, including the genitals, becomes swollen and is often conspicuously coloured. It has recently been shown that the red colour of the rump of certain species is not itself a sexual signal, though it may increase the visibility of the female sexual swellings by contrast. It is not increased, as are the sexual swellings, by the administration of sex hormones, at any rate in rhesus monkeys. But it does act "as a signal suppressing threat by an attacker". 'Seeing red' in monkeys and apes has, therefore, the opposite significance from that usually attributed to this phenomenon in men and bulls.[29] When in heat, females may cross

53

both group boundaries and status boundaries. That is, whatever her normal rank, a female in heat may leave her usual companions and make for a high-ranking male to whom she would not normally have access, or penetrate and be tolerated within a foreign group. Both rhesus monkeys and chimpanzees show what may justifiably be called a increase in 'self-confidence' when in heat; and may also become more aggressive to other females. In this state they present to males of whom they are normally frightened without fear; and the readiness to fight on the part of the male is suppressed by the sexual invitation.

Thus it is not surprising that this gesture of presentation, originally wholly sexual, becomes used as a means of indicating friendliness or submission, since it has the effect of suppressing aggression in the animal to whom presentation is made. It thus becomes the equivalent of human bowing, which indicates submission; or shaking hands, which originally signified that one was carrying no weapon, and hence was friendly. People who keep cats will recognize that when a cat greets the owner by rubbing up against his legs, purring, and at the same time erecting her tail and displaying her ano-genital region, she is using presentation as a means of indicating both friendliness and submission.

Although presentation, in origin, is a female gesture, when used for non-sexual purposes it is shown by females in any stage of the oestrus cycle, by young animals of both sexes, and even by adult males. Presentation as a submissive gesture in both males and females in response to higher-ranking individuals has been described in at least fourteen different species of monkeys. An interesting demonstration of its extended use is named 'protected threat'. If a monkey wants to attack another but dare not do so, he may at the same time threaten his opponent and present to a high-ranking male. This sometimes has the effect of making the high-ranking male do his fighting for him, just as a small boy at school may enlist the aid of a big boy to deal with a tormentor on his behalf.

Presentation, therefore, is an example of a female sexual action which, in a purely social situation, has come to signify submission or greeting.

In exactly the same way, male sexual actions in non-sexual, social settings imply dominance or aggression as a rule, though they may also signify greeting in certain contexts. When one monkey presents, as a gesture of submission, the other will often mount him or her as a gesture of dominance. One observer has alleged that dominance mounting can be distinguished from truly sexual mounting by the fact that in the former activity the mounting animal keeps his feet on the ground, which he does not do when the action is sexual. This observation, however, has not been confirmed. Just as presentation, a female action, may be performed by either sex, so mounting, a male action, is also performed by both sexes when dominance rather than coitus is in question. It is also alleged that, in one species of baboon, an obviously dominant individual may use a submissive action to reassure subordinates, thus handicapping himself. The squirrel monkey who wants to show dominance does so, not by mounting, but by thrusting his erect penis in the other monkey's face. Females, though obviously not possessing a penis, may use a male type of display for the same purpose. The same species may also use penile display as a greeting.

That male sexuality and aggression are intimately linked is supported by the fact that, in a number of species, copulation can be induced by rage; for instance, at the withdrawal of food, or by shock in response to the introduction of a stuffed lynx into the cage. Such copulations may be what is called redirected activities, a substitution of copulation for attacking the withdrawer of food, just as biting the carpet may be a substitute for hitting one's boss. If no female is present, the frustrated animal may masturbate or make coital movements with erect penis *in vacuo*. It is possible, however, though not mentioned by the ethologist from whom this information is taken,[30] that sexual activity, especially after shock, may not be redirected rage, but a reassurance mechanism. In human behaviour, it has often been observed that after a disaster such as a hurricane, or earthquake, or an imagined invasion from Mars, promiscuous sexual activity serves as both a diversion and a reassurance.

In some animals the testes usually descend into the scrotum only during courtship. This is true of the guinea-pig; but it also uses this mechanism as a threat, displaying the descended testes to a rival, when there is no question of copulation. Genital display is also used to warn off intruders; and, in a troop of baboons, a number of males may often be seen acting as sentinels on the periphery of the group. These sentinels sit in such a way that their brightly coloured genitals are clearly visible. Their function appears to be to act as markers of the group's territory, and thus to warn off other baboon troops which may approach.

Another way of marking territory, common to many species, is by the expulsion of urine, an activity closely related to male sexuality. In humans, of course, the voiding of urine may take place as an accompaniment of fear: it may also be used as a gesture of contempt, as when, so Masters reports, the women of a North-West Frontier tribe urinate in the face of a spread-eagled captured enemy. In dogs, tree or lamp-post marking is a gesture of male display and confidence; but in fear situations, dogs may suddenly revert to urinating in inappropriate places like puppies.

Enough has been said to show that, in species other than man, sexual behaviour patterns are habitually used for non-sexual, social purposes which may range from the affirmation of dominance and submission to friendly greeting or merely the inhibition of threat and aggression.

In human beings also many sexual behaviour patterns are used for non-sexual purposes. The Roman Emperor Hadrian built a wall across the northern part of Britain to provide a barrier against the marauding tribes of Picts and Scots. Much of this wall still survives; and in one of the forts I was able to photograph a stone upon which an unmistakable phallus and testicles had been carved, pointing outwards as a threat against potential intruders. A special type of sculpture consisting of a square stone pillar surmounted by a bearded head and bearing in front an erect phallus and testicles were in common use in ancient Athens as boundary markers or house-guards, protecting dwellings and temples. The head was usually that of the god Hermes, and these statues are known as ithyphallic Hermes. We are all familiar with the fact that Freud stated, in *The Interpretation of Dreams* that "All elongated objects, such as sticks, tree-trunks and umbrellas (the opening of these last being comparable to an erection) may stand for the male organ—as well as all long, sharp weapons, such as knives, daggers and pikes."[31] Freud always seems to have treated the penis as an irreducible reality for which many other things might stand, never seeming to realize that the penis itself might signify something other than sexuality. Moreover, as has often been observed, Freudian theory fails to account for those dreams in which the sexual organs appear undisguised. Yet, just as that phallic symbol, a king's sceptre, is indicative of his royal power, so the penis itself, in ancient and franker times, was used as a symbol of authority, or as a magical, aggressive threat to ward off enemies. It is alleged that Jung once made the classic remark: "After all, the penis is only a phallic symbol." Whether he actually said this or not, he certainly ought to have done so.

The sexual offence known as indecent exposure comprises about one third of all sexual offences.[32] Although the exhibitionist may sometimes obtain a modicum of sexual satisfaction by masturbating after his act of exposure, it is clear that the majority of these offenders do not intend or hope for a sexual contact with those to whom they expose themselves. What they intend to provoke is a reaction of horror, disgust, or shock. Exhibitionism is an extremely primitive way of gaining recognition as a male, and is more concerned with obtaining acknowledgment of power than with seeking sexual pleasure. This is borne out by the fact that, in approximately 50 per cent of cases, the females to whom the offender exposes himself are under sixteen; and thus more likely to be shocked or horrified than sexually aroused. This interpretation is also supported by the findings that exhibitionists come predominantly from families in which the mother is over-dominant or over-protective. It is those who feel themselves to be powerless who have to display signal evidence of their power. According to one investigation "The exhibitionists seem to have an inordinate need to please or to be appreciated by significant figures in their early lives. They had difficulty relating to the opposite sex, and often gave indications of covert hostility against females."[33] It might be added that exhibitionism also serves to keep objects at a distance and thus to protect them from suffering sadistic attack. This hostility is, of course, even more obviously manifested in the case of persons whose sexuality is chiefly concerned, not with pleasure, but with sado-masochistic phantasies of dominance-submission relationships.

The conventional psychoanalytic view of sado-masochism is that the sado-masochist has "kept conscious and even exaggerated a part of his infantile sexuality, in order to facilitate the repression of its more objectionable parts".[34] Sadism is conceived as a reassurance mechanism against the threat of castration. If a person is able to do to others what he fears may be done to him, he no longer needs to be afraid. In the same way, masochists invite injuries and humiliations of all kinds except for injury to the genitals; a device of substituting a lesser evil for a greater. But a number of writers seem to feel that it is not easy to fit sado-masochism into psychoanalytic theory, and this is certainly true of Freud himself in his earliest writings on the subject. In *Three Essays on the Theory of Sexuality*, he writes: "The sexuality of most male human beings contains an element of aggressiveness—a desire to subjugate; the biological significance of it seems to lie in the need for overcoming the resistance of the sexual object by means other than the process of wooing. Thus sadism would correspond to an aggressive component of the sexual instinct which has become independent and exaggerated and, by displacement, has usurped the leading position."[35] I am not convinced by this explanation, partly because I do not share Freud's somewhat Victorian view that women have such a resistance to or distaste for sex that they have to be vanquished by means other than wooing. This is not to deny that many women like a man to show a modicum of strength in sexual behaviour, which may increase their excitement, but need not be anything to do with resistance. Later in the same book, Freud writes "The history of human civilization shows beyond any doubt that there is an intimate connection between cruelty and the sexual instinct; but nothing has been done towards explaining the connection, apart from laying emphasis on the aggressive factor in the libido. . . . All that need be said is that no satisfactory explanation of this perversion has been put forward and that it seems possible that a number of mental impulses are combined in it to produce a single resultant."[36]

From time to time Freud refers to an 'instinct for

mastery'. He relates the 'impulse of cruelty' to this; and in another passage relates it also to cannibalistic impulses concerned with what he calls the satisfaction of "the other, and ontogenetically, the older of the great instinctual needs". In another passage, in the 20th Introductory lecture, he refers to "the puzzling sadists".[37] In his paper on "The Economic Problem of Masochism" he refers to his later concept of the death instinct turned outwards as aggression towards the external world. It "is then called the destructive instinct, the instinct for mastery, or the will to power".[38]

It took the world war of 1914-18 to convince Freud that there was any necessity to postulate an independent aggressive drive of any kind; and I have written elsewhere about the possible reasons for this. In the specific field which we are here considering, I think Freud's tardy recognition of the will to power is still bedevilling our thinking. We can see from animal behaviour how sexual behaviour is 'borrowed' to serve other functions. If Freud had fully recognized the importance of dominance behaviour and the will to power in human beings at an earlier stage in his thinking, I believe that he might have formulated his views on sado-masochism both differently and more clearly.

The Kronhausens reckon that 80 per cent of pornographic literature is sado-masochistic. Most of this literature is concerned far more with dominance and submission than with sensual pleasure. As Steven Marcus writes in *The Other Victorians*: "In both 'My Secret Life' and pornography, it is often extremely difficult to distinguish one woman from another; finally

61

they are all the same, although the search for variety and the quantitative accumulation of experiences mechanically persists. And there is also in both the final absence of all emotions except the aggressive ones."[39] In another passage, Mr Marcus writes of pornography as "a literature obsessed with pleasure and yet unpleasurable, whose aim is said to be pleasure, although it is a pleasure from which the actuality of gratification is excluded, and whose impulse toward totality is the equivalent of obliteration. It is, I suppose, possible to explain the kind of sexual writings we are discussing strictly according to the pleasure principle, as it undergoes the usual procedures of distortion. I do not think, however, that its distinct unpleasurableness, its violence and aggressiveness, its impulse towards extinction are satisfactorily explained by that principle alone." Nor do I.

In America, and Great Britain, there is freely available an English translation of a French pornographic novel entitled *Histoire d'O*,[40] or the Story of O, as it is called in English. The authorship of this work is disputed, although it has been attributed to various well-known persons, both male and female. The theme of the book is, exclusively, male dominance. 'O' is made to submit to men by beatings, humiliations and so on. She is not allowed any independence of her own, not even to the extent of being allowed the freedom of her own body. Her clothes, behaviour, make-up, occupation—all are dictated by whatever master she is assigned to. It is no accident that she is called 'O' for she is literally nothing in her own right; she is merely a product of male sexual phantasy. And in this work, as in the books of an earlier date which he studied, Steven Marcus's point holds good. There is very little emphasis on pleasure. Although 'O' is alleged to obtain pleasure from total submission, there is no joy in her slavery; only a kind of distorted sense of her own significance as being a participant in greater reality, that of her ruthless master. Obviously we all know that there is an attraction in the oceanic feeling of being merged in a greater reality than ourselves, whether this be in a crowd, in the Deity, or in certain forms of experience of music or art. As Fenichel puts it: "Certain narcissistic feelings of well-being are characterised by the fact that they are felt as a reunion with an omnipotent force in the external world brought about either by incorporating parts of this world, or by the fantasy of being incorporated by it. Religious ecstasy, patriotism, and similar feelings are characterised by the ego's participation in something unattainably high."[41] But of course such participation is at the expense of identity. It is indeed reducing the individual to a cipher, making a person into nothing but an 'O'.

Another illustration of the point I am making can be culled from a study of the perversion known as paedophilia. Although many factors, including proximity, recent sexual trauma or deprivation, intelligence and other things, may determine the sexual selection of a child as a sexual object, it is surely obvious that considerations of dominance must be important in most cases. A child is chosen as the recipient of advances because the offender does not feel powerful enough in himself to obtain what he wants from an adult. In a child-adult relationship a dominance structure is built-in, by virtue of the adult's superior strength and size. The weak, insecure, immature adult, in approaching a child, feels relieved of the burden of having to compete on equal terms, or of asserting himself as an adult male in such a way as to obtain an adult female response. In many animal societies, as we have seen, it is the most dominant males who have the first access to the females; and indeed, in a number of species, there are always a large number of superfluous males who are not dominant enough to get access to females at all, and who therefore perforce remain celibate. In other words, the establishment of a place in the dominance hierarchy *precedes* the attainment of sexual satisfaction; and if efforts at obtaining a place fail so that the individual is graded near the bottom of the pecking order the penalty is that he remains unmated. It is for this reason that pornographic literature and the sexual perversions are much more concerned with dominance than with pleasure. The pervert is essentially a person who has never been able to establish himself on equal terms with other males or feel that he can compete with them. Hence his main preoccupation is not with sexuality as pleasurable fulfilment, but with the necessary precursory establishment of a dominant status. Only when this has been achieved is he free to enjoy sexuality.

It is my contention that the bulk of pornography, and much of what we call perverse sexual behaviour, is not primarily concerned with sex at all, but with dominance.

This precursory element in sado-masochistic phantasy can, according to Helene Deutsch, also be detected in the rape phantasies of pubescent girls. She writes: "Often the phantasy is divided into two acts: the first, the masochistic act, produces the sexual tension, and the second, the amorous act, supplies all the delights of being loved and desired. These fantasies vanish with the giving up of masturbation and yield to erotic infatuations detached from direct sexuality."[42]

It is also appropriate to note the view of Karen Horney in this connection. "Sadism and masochism have fundamentally nothing whatsoever to do with intercourse, but the female role in intercourse (being penetrated) *lends* itself more readily to a personal misinterpretation (when needed) of masochistic performance; and the male role, to one of sadistic activity."[43]

In the same category of observation is Freud's discovery that many children misinterpret the sexual act as an attack by the male upon the female. Children, in spite of infantile masturbation, have little idea of sexual pleasure; but they have a lively concept of dominance-submission relations, since they are engaged perpetually in struggles to establish status in relation to their parents, rivalry with siblings and contemporaries, and all the manifold phantasy activity of childhood which is concerned with being as big, as strong, as powerful as the feared and envied adults who surround them.

The whole emphasis of conventional psychoanalysis has been upon infantile *sexuality*, and the extent to which the persistence of infantile sexual constellations interfere with the establishment of adult genitality. But I think it just as likely, in fact much more likely, that the primary difficulty which children experience is in establishing a sense of their own power and a place in the human hierarchy, and that their sexual difficulties are secondary to this, not primary.

Let us examine a few examples from clinical experience. In spite of our so-called enlightenment, hysterical frigidity in women is still a common symptom. In conventional psychoanalytic psychopathology, hysterics have remained at the phallic phase of sexual development. "Hysterical individuals have either never overcome their early object choice, or else were so fixated on it that after a dispapointment in later life they return to it. Because all sexuality comes to represent to them the infantile incestuous love, the urge to repress the Oedipus complex represses all sexuality."[44] Thus, hysterics tend to exclude their genitals and genital sensation from their body image, because all intercourse represents intercourse with the father. However, one can equally well look at it with a slightly different emphasis. Hysterics are still in a stage when they regard themselves as weak, and others as strong, just as they did, quite reasonably, when they were children. They also regard intercourse as an attack by the male upon the female; think of sexual activity in terms of yielding or submitting, instead of as a cooperative pleasure; and are protecting themselves from experiencing any genital sensation at all because they conceive of such sensation as likely to be painful rather than a pleasure. It is certainly true that, in one sense, hysterics conceive of intercourse as intercourse with the father or a father substitute; since they conceive of themselves as weak children, and their partners as powerful adults; but it is not so much guilt about Oedipal wishes which prevents them responding, as the fear of being hurt by a much more powerful adult; a fear which has often been reinforced in childhood by actual physical punishment. To my mind an interpretation of hysterical frigidity in terms of power relations is at least as convincing as one in terms of Oedipal sexual guilt.

If we turn from the fearful, shrinking type of hysterical woman to consider the *femme fatale*, the point I am trying to make becomes even more obvious. Whether or not they are actually frigid, *femmes fatales* are using their feminine attractions for dominance purposes rather than for love, of which they are not fully capable. The type is archetypally portrayed by the Princess Turandot, heroine of Puccini's opera of that name. As convention demands, Turandot is endowed with great beauty. As a Princess of China, the man who wins her wins the Imperial throne. So she has to be sure that he is worthy of such an honour, and thus contrives a test which he must pass which, conventionally enough, consists of three riddles to which he must give correct answers. Those who fail to pass the test are put to death; and the list of executed suitors is a long one. The last riddle put by Turandot to the intrepid Prince of Tartary who dares to woo her is as follows: "What is the ice that sets you on fire?" to which the answer is, of course, herself, the Princess Turandot. Frigidity has only been better exemplified to me by the first psychotic woman I ever saw, who complained that her vagina contained a block of ice. When Turandot's lover finally kisses her,

"her strength is gone, and with it all thought of revenge, all her fierceness and courage".[45] Only when she can pass beyond her sado-masochistic preoccupation with domination is she able to experience the pleasure of love.

In clinical practice ladies like Turandot are all too common. They are generally supposed to be suffering from penis envy; which, according to Freud, is universal, leaves "ineradicable traces on their development and the formation of their character and which will not be surmounted in even the most favourable cases without a severe expenditure of psychical energy".[46] Karen Horney, who was notoriously dissatisfied with Freud's formulation, writes that "an assertion that one half of the human race is discontented with the sex assigned to it and can overcome this discontent only in favourable circumstances—is decidedly unsatisfying, not only to feminine narcissism but also to biological science".[47] However, if we take penis envy not as primarily sexual, but as pseudo-sexual, the state of mind of the little girl becomes much more comprehensible. It is not that she is dissatisfied with being female as such, but that she is discontented with being, as all children are, comparatively powerless. In her quest for dominance, she comes across the fact that boys are, as numerous experiments have shown, innately more aggressive than girls. Direct observation of children's play has shown a sex difference of this kind from as early as two years old. Males are therefore conceived, quite correctly, to be potentially more powerful than girls; and the symbol of masculine power is quite obviously the penis. In my view we ought not to talk about penis envy, but about phallic envy; a semantic distinction which may seem pedantic, but which actually conveys an important shift in emphasis. "After all, the penis is only a phallic symbol."

So long as the child, or the childish adult, feels him or herself to be at a disadvantage in the dominance hierarchy, so long will both sexes show phallic envy and tend to identify with the more powerful male. But the price of being thus preoccupied is to be excluded from the pleasures of love. I should like to put forward the hypothesis that the more neurotic a person is, the more will he or she be preoccupied with status, and the more will his or her sexuality be distorted to serve dominance-submission purposes rather than the end of obtaining pleasure. It is interesting to speculate upon what kind of psychopathology we should have learned if Freud had paid as much attention to his 'instinct for mastery' as he did to sex. I think he would have concluded that many sexual disturbances are secondary to the most striking peculiarity of the human being; the enormously prolonged period of his childhood, and hence of his dependency. We might even have had a book entitled 'Beyond the Power Principle' if Freud had recognized that power comes before pleasure as I am postulating.

Since, in early childhood, the male is actually more aggressive and dominant than the female, it often takes longer for the girl than for the boy to become fully confident in her sexual role. This is not so much because it is a man's world as because, for many women, fulfilment and feminine status are only finally achieved by the production of children, which often comes relatively late in life. Many perfectly normal little girls spend a good proportion of their childhood wishing to be boys without any disastrous after-effects upon their subsequent relations with men. The same is not true for boys who wish to be girls; and in my opinion the tolerance with which tomboy girls are regarded, and the suspicion with which girlish boys are viewed, are amply justified by clinical experience. If one tries to explain difference between the sexes in terms of conventional psychoanalytic psychopathology, it is all too easy to get lost in a mass of speculation. If, however, one accepts that both sexes use masculine sexual symbolism as an expression of their striving for status there is no difficulty in understanding this interesting sexual difference.

In adult life, women who are chiefly motivated by the desire for power are regarded as more emotionally disturbed than males who are similarly driven. Of course we are all familiar with the bossy, aggressive, ambitious woman who is envious of men, destructive towards them, and who is clearly aping men in an unsatisfactory and tiresome way. Yet I do not believe that all women in powerful positions are necessarily eaten up with penis envy. Lionel Tiger, in his book *Men in Groups* makes the interesting point that "one common way in which females acquire high office is by being close and politically active relatives of senior politicians who die. This is perhaps the most obvious and certainly the easiest way in which women have come to occupy high posts."[48] Women who attain political power may, in many instances, be fearsomely 'phallic' and competitive. But I am willing to consider that some may be following a basic pattern amongst other primates in which the females associated with the most dominant males themselves acquire dominant status without having to compete with the male or strive in a masculine manner.

If we consider sado-masochism in its wider context as pseudo-sex and an expression of the status struggle, we find that, in early life, the human female is equally interested in dominance, but that she has a particular way of learning to exercise power which is indirect. That is, because of the male's superior strength, she learns to influence him in ways which are not directly competitive, but which are none the less effective. Getting round people, cajoling them, exercising diplomacy, and charming them are all feminine ways of exerting influence which we all accept and to which we all respond. Hysterics are often accused, quite rightly, of manipulating people, and this characteristic is generally held to be one reason why hysterics are irritating, since it is supposed that no one likes being manipulated in an underhand way. However, I venture to suggest that men do not in fact mind being manipulated by normal, affectionate women who know how to get round them. It is the essential falsity of the hysterical type of manipulation which is irritating: the realization that her manœuvres are a disguise for competitiveness, and her apparent charm a mask for envy. In *Anxiety and Neurosis* Charles Rycroft writes: "All the hysterics whom I have treated, both the men and the women, have gone through childhoods which have left them deeply convinced of their own insignificance and that their parents have been primarily preoccupied with their own lives and not with those of their children." In another passage he refers to the hysteric as having "felt herself overshadowed by persons more forceful than herself", and of "having been defeated and forced into a submissive role, which leaves the victim feeling consciously helpless and inadequate and unconsciously envious and resentful"[49]. It is evident that the author agrees with my view of the struggle in childhood, and lays less emphasis than most Freudians upon the vicissitudes of infantile sexuality.

We began this discussion of sado-masochism in answer to a question: "Is human cruelty really a sexual phenomenon?" From what I have written above, it is obvious that the answer must be "No", even though it may be true that cruelty releases and makes possible sexual experience for those perverts who require extreme reassurance as to their own strength and their victim's weakness before they can be potent. In such men as Neville Heath and Ian Brady, one mechanism which is operating, apart from the psychopathic absence of control, is certainly an extreme sense of insignificance, neglect and humiliation, which makes the exercise of physical power over another both reassuring and exciting; and the acme of physical power over another is the act of murder. When snakes engage in ritual battles the loser removes himself from the scene and is apparently unable to engage in sexual activity for some weeks. The victor, on the other hand, celebrates his triumph by an immediate mating. Human males do not generally have to win a ritual contest before they can engage in sexual intercourse; but they do require to possess some sense of their own power and strength, some confidence in their own physical capacities. Persons who require the assistance of sado-masochistic phantasies before they can perform the sexual act, or who actually have to engage in sadistic activities, are persons who have no such confidence. Essentially, they believe themselves to be weak and helpless children, and other people to be grown-up and much more powerful; a belief which persists emotionally in spite of actual evidence to the contrary. Their sado-masochistic preoccupations reflect a failure to achieve an established place in a real and actual hierarchical structure with other human beings; a step which appears to be an essential prerequisite to becoming capable of a true love involvement.

Although, as I have written above, there are a few psychopathic people who act out their sadistic phantasies, by far the majority of patients who consult a psychiatrist on account of such phantasies are, in real life, passive, ingratiating and fearful of women. Their phantasy life, split off from reality, contains in exaggerated and distorted form the active and dominant aspects of their masculinity which have been repressed and dissociated.

Neurotics of this kind are generally ashamed of, and horrified by their own sadistic preoccupations. Although it is conceivable that some such people, egged on by authorities who encourage sadistic behaviour, might be persuaded to act out their phantasies, it is not probable. Persons with a psychopathic or paranoid character structure are, paradoxically, much more likely to behave cruelly than the passive or alienated male who is internally preoccupied with sadistic imaginations. For the imagination luxuriates when action is rendered impossible. The Marquis de Sade wrote most of his pornography—and his philosophy—when imprisoned in the Bastille. Although it is true that he did act out his phantasies to a minor extent in ill-treating prostitutes, it is unlikely that we should possess the dubious pleasure of being able to read *Les 120 journées de Sodome* or *La Nouvelle Justine* if he had not, for eleven years, been confined in prison. As Simone de Beauvoir writes: "It was not murder that fulfilled Sade's erotic nature; it was literature." In another passage she postulates, rightly in my view, that Sade's sadism was a gigantic compensation for his inability to become emotionally intoxicated. "The curse which weighed upon Sade—and which only his childhood could explain—was this 'autism' which prevented him from ever forgetting himself or being genuinely aware of the reality of the other person."[50] People who are sufficiently worried by their sado-masochistic inclinations to consult a psychiatrist generally have ample reason in their background to account for their problems, and fit well enough into the general assumption that it is the experience of early childhood which has given rise to their abnormality. If they respond satisfactorily to treatment, their sadistic impulses cease to disturb them *pari passu* with the development of a more active, dominant attitude to life.

I think we are justified in concluding that cruelty is not primarily a sexual phenomenon. Indeed, I hope I have succeeded in demonstrating that sado-masochism is less 'sexual' than is generally supposed, and is really a 'pseudo-sexual' activity or preoccupation, much more concerned with power relations than with pleasure.

The relation of cruelty with sexuality is often misunderstood. Do the riot police have erections when they are dragging students from ambulances or clubbing them? It is highly improbable. Yet we have to recognize that, at a physiological level, there is a close connection between anger and sexuality. In his book *Sexual Behavior in the Human Female* Kinsey draws attention to the fact that the state of the body in sexual arousal and its condition in anger are closely similar. He lists fourteen physiological changes which occur when a man is sexually excited, including blood pressure, pulse rate, alteration in peripheral circulation and so on. All these fourteen changes are common to both the state of anger and to the state of sexual arousal. Indeed, he can only find four other physiological phenomena which are not so, but which are peculiar to sexual arousal.[51] This being so, it is not difficult to understand that men and women respond to the portrayal of violence with an excitement which is closely linked experientially with sexuality. Indeed, a modicum of introspection reveals this. When one is sexually aroused, one has an enhanced sense of vitality. Muscular strength is actually increased, with a consequent feeling of power. There is an experience of well-being, of vital participation in life which is so important a part of existence that we are apt to look in pity upon those members of our species who may never have been fully awakened sexually. Although cruelty is not generally, I believe, a sexual phenomenon, yet the study of sado-masochism is important to our theme.

For 'pseudo-sex' is predominantly concerned with power relationships, and so is human cruelty: a phenomenon which can only be understood if we take into account the fact that many people suffer from persistent feelings of powerlessness and helplessness which date from a very early period of childhood.

I wrote above that people who consult a psychiatrist on account of sado-masochistic preoccupations have usually had a childhood in which their emotional needs were not fully met, or in which they were actually neglected, unwanted, or unloved. As we have seen, the same is true of most, though not of all, psychopaths. But how far are we justified in assuming that human beings who are, or who wish to be, cruel have all had unsatisfactory childhoods which have left them full of resentment?

At an earlier point in this essay, when discussing the Russells' theory that violence is invariably a response to stress, I wrote that there was no doubt that the propensity to violence was much accentuated by the ill-effects of an unhappy childhood. People who have had no love, or not enough; people who have been deprived by death of one or both parents; people who have suffered cruelty or indifference in their earliest years—all these undoubtedly carry with them into adult life a load of resentment which they may 'take out' upon others if they have the opportunity. It is a truism that bullies have generally been bullied; and we are familiar enough with the psychological mechanism of displacement to take it for granted that resentment can often be directed towards substitutes; so that innocent persons may come in for violence which should more appropriately have been directed at parents.

Yet this psychiatric explanation of man's cruelty remains unsatisfactory for the simple reason that it is fairly easy to make people who do not appear to have had unusually unhappy childhoods behave cruelly, as the experiments already quoted of S. Milgram demonstrate. Sadistic behaviour in totalitarian states especially, though not only in them, is so common that not all who indulge in it can possibly be labelled as abnormal. The concentration camps have shown that it is not difficult to train people without obvious psychiatric symptomatology to become first indifferent to cruelty, and then to enjoy its exercise. It may be that those in concentration camps who refused to participate in barbarities were more 'abnormal', or at least unusual, than those who did not. To be an Eichmann is less rare than to be a saint.

We are faced with what appear to be incompatible statements. There is good reason to assume that those who have had deprived unhappy childhoods are likely to be cruel, because they carry with them into adult life a burden of hatred and resentment. Yet normal people can also be persuaded to be cruel without much difficulty. Since, by definition, normal people may be assumed to have had a sufficiently happy infancy and childhood to render them free of any marked proclivity to hatred, it looks as if these statements are irreconcilable. Should one, therefore, discard the whole edifice of psychoanalytic research and theory, and suppose, not only that human beings are naturally cruel, but that their cruelty is unrelated to infantile and childhood experience?

Since I am an analyst, I have a declared interest in preserving at least some parts of analytic theory. It does not make sense to me to suppose that childhood experience has little influence on development: or that cruelty is unrelated to deprivation and neglect. Clinical experience has convinced me that people who are, or who wish to be, cruel are often revenging themselves in the present for feelings of being disregarded in the past: and that the emotionally lamed who are unable to give and receive love because they have not experienced it, are envious and resentful of those who are able to love and be loving. It is, of course, obvious that no child has a perfect upbringing; and it therefore follows that everyone is likely to have some resentments towards parents or other authorities which may be taken out on enemies in later life. Nevertheless, one might have hoped that most children would have been sufficiently loved and cherished that they would not easily be persuaded that torturing another human being was either acceptable or enjoyable.

Moreover, analysts are being increasingly supported in many of their assumptions by the results of modern research. One of the most interesting developments of our time is the beginning of confirmation of some analytic theory which seemed speculative by the study of both human infants and the young of other species. So much is this true that I believe that anyone who does *not* think that the environment of infancy is an important determinate of future character must be asked to provide some pretty cogent proofs before we need take him seriously. Professor Washburn remarked recently: "We can now say that there is no question that the earliest events in life, in the first year or two, are profoundly important, whether for a young monkey or a human being. This is not something which is generally recognized around the world. Infants are frequently treated with the greatest casualness."[52]

Since it is not reasonable to discard the hypothesis that an unfavourable experience of early childhood is likely to leave persons with an increased propensity for cruelty, and yet we have to accept the fact that so-called normal people can easily be persuaded to behave cruelly, we are still left with a dilemma. There are two ways out of it. We can assume that our habitual ways of rearing babies in our culture are sadly deficient so that what we consider a 'normal' adult is in fact a deprived and damaged adult. Or we can assume that there is some basic flaw in the human species which makes human beings cruel irrespective of how much loving care they have received.

# THE UBIQUITY OF PARANOIA

I think we may be able to gain some illumination if we turn from the consideration of sadists and psychopaths to the study of people with a paranoid type of character structure. It may seem odd that in seeking to understand what we may now call a 'normal' propensity to cruelty, I should invoke the word 'paranoid' which, in the minds of most people, is associated with some of the most severe forms of mental illness. However, as analysts know, and many other people are beginning to realize, paranoid traits can be detected in most of us, and many analysts now refer to the earliest stage of emotional development in infants as the paranoid-schizoid position.

I suppose that if I were to ask most psychiatrists for their first association to the word 'paranoid' they would reply 'projection', and go on to describe that curious, ubiquitous mechanism by which human beings disown what is unacceptable in themselves and attribute it wrongly to someone else. However, projection need not be, though it generally is, of unpleasant characteristics. The idealization which is part of falling in love is a form of projection. So is the misplaced veneration with which we are apt to regard political leaders or other authorities, including our own analysts if we have them. I have known paranoid patients who were convinced that I, behind their backs, was engaging in all kinds of complicated plots and negotiations *for their benefit*. But whether projection is negative or positive, the common feature is that the subject regards other people as possessing great, often magical power for good, or more commonly, ill; and himself as possessing little or no power and being therefore in a weak or helpless position. It is a persistence into adult life of something which we imagine the baby to feel; the sense that he is at the mercy of figures who are much more powerful than himself. Even those of us who are not psychiatrically trained are familiar with the symptoms of a fully developed paranoid psychosis; the delusional systems in which the subject comes to believe that he is the centre of malignant attention from groups of enemies, that his thoughts are being interfered with, that he is being tortured by mysterious machines and so on. We may imagine that so-called normal people could never come to believe anything so ludicrous as the delusional systems of the insane. Yet the evidence suggests that normal people can, without much difficulty, be persuaded to accept the most absurd calumnies about supposed enemies. Delusional beliefs about witches, Negroes, Jews and other minority groups or categories have been accepted throughout history by persons of high intelligence who could not possibly be considered insane.

In 1486 appeared the first edition of the *Malleus Maleficarum*, the Hammer of Witches, written by two Inquisitors of the Catholic Church named Heinrich Kramer and James Sprenger. This is a kind of manual for witch-hunters, designed to instruct the uninitiated in what witchcraft is about, and to issue minute instructions as to how witches should be proceeded against, including what tortures should be used and when. The whole book is a fascinating and horrifying manual of psychopathology, which demonstrates how easily men can build up delusional systems about women. Witchcraft is held to be responsible for many disorders in men which we should now call neurotic, especially for impotence. According to the authors, "Three general vices appear to have special dominion over wicked women, namely infidelity, ambition, and lust. Therefore they are more than others inclined toward witchcraft, who more than others are given to these vices. . . . Now there are as it is said in the Papal Bull, seven methods by which they infect with witchcraft the venereal act and the conception of the womb. First, by inclining the minds of men to inordinate passion; second, by obstructing their generative force; third, by removing the members accommodated to that act; fourth, by changing men into beasts by their magic art; fifth, by destroying the generative force in women; sixth, by procuring abortion; seventh, by offering children to devils besides other animals and fruits of the earth with which they work much harm."[53] The authors give many examples of what they call "diabolic operations with regard to the male organ". There is, for example, a marvellous story about a witch who made a collection of penises and stored them in a church tower. Such tales would be amusing if one did not recall the persecution and torture of innocent women which these phantasies prompted. The introduction to *Malleus Maleficarum* by one recent translator, the Revd. Montague Summers, is itself notable in that it reveals his own beliefs. This monstrous, horrifying farrago of paranoid delusions is referred to as "the most solid, the most important work in the whole library of witchcraft". It is alleged to contain "seemingly inexhaustible wells of wisdom". "What is most surprising is the modernity of the book. There is hardly a problem, a complex, a difficulty, which they have not foreseen, and discussed, and resolved. Here are cases which occur in the law-courts today, set out with the greatest clarity, argued with unflinching logic, and judged with scrupulous impartiality. . . . The *Malleus Maleficarum* is one of the world's few books written *sub specie aeternitatis*."

One would like to think that Montague Summers was unique in taking pathological phantasy for fact, but a more modern example, concerned with anti-Semitism rather than witchcraft, demonstrates how easy it is to persuade large numbers of people of the existence of conspiracy where in fact there is none.

In *Warrant for Genocide* Norman Cohn examines the effect produced by the circulation of that malicious forgery known as "The Protocols of the Elders of Zion". Even so sober a journal as the London *Times* was, in the 'twenties, constrained to remark that there might be something in the idea that there was an international group of Jewish financiers plotting the ruin of Europe; and many of the thrillers of the 'twenties seem to have been based on this phantasy. "Have we been struggling these tragic years to blow up and extirpate the secret organization of German world dominion only to find beneath it another, more dangerous because more secret. . . . The Elders of Zion as represented in their Protocols are by no means kinder taskmasters than William II and his henchmen would have been."[54] This comes from *The Times* of May

83

8th, 1920. The following week the *Spectator* devoted a long review and an editorial to the Jewish Peril, and later in the year demanded that a Royal Commission should be set up to investigate the possibility of a world-wide conspiracy under Jewish leadership. Even a superficial glance at the large body of literature dealing with colour prejudice uncovers a vast nexus of irrational belief about the Negro which is delusional; but which is accepted so easily by so many people that to talk of delusions being the prerogative of the insane becomes nonsensical. Of course there is little doubt that people who lynch Negroes, or who show particularly violent prejudice against them, are themselves deprived and injured, and thus welcome the provision of a scapegoat whom they can despise as less than themselves, and whom they can blame for their own faults. But scapegoats are welcome to men and women who are not obviously abnormal; and colour prejudice is admitted by many intelligent and apparently well-balanced individuals who show no particular sign of mental instability.

Indeed, it may be more 'natural' for societies to have out-groups who receive the paranoid projection of the majority, as in the examples of the untouchables of India, and the outcasts of Japan, although some authorities dispute this.

In less extreme form, embryonic 'delusions' can be detected in all of us when we start to speculate about the habits and beliefs of persons belonging to a different stratum of society, or adhering to a different religion from our own. I know of no evidence that 'the poor' kept coals in the bath, when they had one. Yet in the 'twenties, it was widely believed that they did. The stereotypes we are all too ready to attach to the Irish, the Welsh, the Scots, or to Catholics may simply attest our lazy habits of generalization. But most of our thought-less labels are pejorative, and indicate our pleasure at finding some other group not only different from, but supposedly inferior to, ourselves. Although we may admire the Scottish passion for education, it is with relief that we recall their over-serious pedantry. The Irish may be poetic; but at the price of fecklessness and alcoholism. The Welsh are fine singers; but apt to be dishonest and dirty (Taffy was a Welshman . . .). As for Catholics; we all know that they are in a gigantic conspiracy to restore England to the true faith and cannot be trusted to keep an oath of allegiance to the Queen, since loyalty to the Pope is paramount.

Of course, beliefs and prejudices often have some small basis in reality, just as the paranoid projections of the insane generally have some original connection with truth. Paranoid psychotics are often aware of hostility from other people which does exist: their failure is to perceive that love and respect can co-exist with this hostility. The Jews were not engaged in an international conspiracy; but the Rothschilds, by financing needy governments, did in fact exert a powerful influence.

However, there can be very few of us who do not, unthinkingly, entertain beliefs or prejudices about groups other than our own which will not stand the light of critical examination. A proportion of these beliefs and prejudices are positive, just as a few paranoid projections are. But by far the majority are negative,

Bradford College Library
Bradford, Massachusetts 01830

critical, or condemnatory; for it is prejudices of this kind which serve to bolster our self-esteem, just as the delusions of the full-blown psychotic make him out to be of immense importance, and his persecutors as wicked rogues.

I think that the tendency of human beings, unlike other animals, to pursue their enemies to the death and to treat them with cruelty, is intimately associated with paranoid projection. One of the features of a full-blown paranoid delusional system is the conviction that the persecutors have magical powers against which the subject is relatively helpless. If, therefore, one does finally get one's enemy in one's power, he must be utterly destroyed. In addition, it is tempting to retaliate and to prove one's shakily superior power by torturing and humiliating him. Into this man's capacity for identification also enters. There would be little point in torturing an enemy if we could not enter imaginatively into his agony. There can be no doubt that we wish to behave to persecutors as we believe or fear that they would behave to us. Directly our paranoid potential is aroused, it is as if we set foot into a mythological world inhabited, not by human beings, but by demons, ogres and witches whose evil practices can only be combated by equal malice on our own part. Of course, when we enter that other state in which projection plays such a marked part, the state which Freud called 'the psychosis of normal people' and which is better known as the state of being 'in love', we also enter a mythological world which suddenly seems transformed by the magical influence of the beloved into a place of sweetness and light inhabited by only the kindliest and most noble of persons.

'Falling in love' is generally recognized as being a common state of mind, and, in spite of Freud's diagnostic label, is not considered abnormal. Its opposite, 'falling in hate' is not so widely acknowledged. Yet I believe it to be about as common, and a great deal more dangerous. Both states of mind belong to a very early stage of emotional development in which 'good' and 'bad' are widely separated absolutes. It is the paranoid-schizoid stage of development, before the so-called depressive position appears, in which good and bad are recognized as attributes of the same person.

In recent years, a number of writers have been questioning whether man, although so successful as a species, is quite such a biological paragon as he appears. This is partly because we are in obvious danger of exterminating ourselves with nuclear, chemical or biological weapons. It is also because we have failed to find an adequate explanation for the more unpleasant aspects of human nature, preferring the Utopian hope that cruelty and hostility can be eliminated if society were sufficiently modified.

It is likely that an observer from another planet would regard the human species as a biological error. For, although man has become predominant over other animals, he is obviously wildly incompetent in managing his own nature, and in co-operating with those of his fellows who do not belong to his own immediate group. The unrestricted growth of population, the grossly inequitable distribution of wealth, the recurrent phenomenon of war, and the lack of a coherent political system must seem to a Martian evidence that the earth's dominant species is sadly flawed; and that, in terms of the greatest good of the greatest number, the ant and chimpanzee are better adapted. What we might call the 'fatal flaw' in human nature has of course been commented upon by other writers. Some call it original sin; others, like Arthur Koestler[55] postulate a failure of adequate connection between fore-brain and hind-brain; and thus a divorce between reason and emotion: still others write in terms of 'alienation'. Indeed there are few writers who merely echo "What a piece of work is man", and who do not wish for any emendment.

Can we make any attempt to diagnose this fatal flaw in terms of psychoanalytic or any other theory? The biologist, looking at man as one of many species of primate, must at once be struck by certain peculiarities. The first peculiarity is known as neoteny, or foetalization: that is, the retention and prolongation of foetal characteristics into adult life. Man's divergence from other primate stocks is marked by the persistence of features which are typical of the foetal stage of other primates. The distribution of hair on man is, according to Julian Huxley, "extremely similar to that on a late foetus of a chimpanzee, and there can be little doubt that it represents an extension of the temporary anthropoid phase into permanence". The small size of man's teeth and their late eruption is another example; as is the position of his head relative to the body, the flatness of his face, the absence of heavy brow ridges and so on. This 'foetalization' of man is mirrored in the extremely slow rate of his development. "The period from birth to the first onset of sexual maturity comprises nearly a quarter of the normal span of his life, instead of an eighth, tenth or twelfth as in some other animals."[56] This prolongation of immaturity can be seen to some extent in other primates, but is far more marked in man. Just as the attainment of sexual maturity is delayed, so is the development of the brain. A young chimpanzee completes its brain growth within twelve months of birth. Most monkeys complete theirs within six months. Man, on the other hand, has a brain at birth which is only 23 per cent of its adult size; and growth in general is not complete until more than twenty years after birth. It is this fact, of course, together with the enormous development of the neocortex, which accounts for man's intelligence and for his increased capacity for learning. But the increased capacity for learning and the sensitivity for early impressions combined with memory cuts both ways. There is increasing evidence, in part derived from the study of human infants, in part from experiments with the young of other primates, that unfavourable conditioning in infancy produces disastrous results for the future which are certainly long-lasting and may be permanent. Professor Harlow and his associates have carried out a large number of experiments with infant rhesus monkeys which demonstrate that both complete and partial isolation have permanent effects upon the adult's capacity to relate to other monkeys. "Prolonged social isolation progressively depresses any capability of social interaction, probably heightens aggression or perhaps only appears to because it prevents learning of restraints in expressing aggression, and inhibits or destroys heterosexual interaction and maternal capabilities."[57]

Observations of human infants are gradually being accumulated which indicate, beyond reasonable doubt, that the earliest experiences of the baby with its mother have as far-reaching effects as psychoanalysts have postulated from the study of adult psychotics and psychoneurotics.

The human infant is born into the world in a peculiarly helpless condition, and remains in this condition for a longer period, relative to the total life span, than the young of other primates. As Michael Chance has pointed out,[58] the young of monkeys and apes either cling to their mother's fur at birth or else, as in the case of the gorilla, are perpetually cradled by the mother. Continuity of bodily contact is an important reassurance mechanism, and in its absence, there is evidence that human infants develop less satisfactorily than if the mother plays with and handles the infant constantly. Although infant monkeys and apes are highly dependent on the mother, all species, with the exception of the gorilla, show an *active* component in their behaviour in that they actively grasp their mother's fur, and perhaps this is the earliest form of self-assertive or 'aggressive' behaviour. Human infants display a 'grasp' reflex from an early age but there is nothing for them to grasp. Moreover, although, for all we know, they may need as much or more bodily contact than young apes, young mothers have the option, often exercised, of leaving their infants in perambulators or cots for large sections of the day, never picking them up except to feed or bath them. As Professor Harlow writes: "The human neonate is so physically immature that it cannot clasp, cling, and feed back to the mother as effectively as the neonatal monkey, but this does not mean that its early affectional requirements are basically different. The human neonate has the same contactual, nutritional, and protective needs as the monkey, but its immaturity places a heavier burden of responsibility upon the human mother and prolongs the period of dependency."[59] We urgently need more comparative studies of the personality development of infants who have, for example, been constantly carried around on their mother's backs as compared with those who have been left for most of the day on their own.

One such study that shows how very differently infants develop is a comparison of American infants with Ugandans.[60] The American mother leaves her child in a cot. The Ugandan mother carries her child about. The Ugandan baby shows anxiety about separation from the mother as early as six months—two or four months *before* the American. This might be interpreted as indicating that mothers *decrease* infant security by carrying infants about. On the other hand, analysts believe that the earliest months are of vital importance; and that, if an infant shows this early anxiety, it at least means that the mother has become important at a critical early period. Commenting on this study, Mussen, Conger and Kagan make the following comment: "The Uganda baby is with his mother almost continuously, so we should expect him to regard the mother as an essential part of every situation. Her absence elicits a discrepancy that elicits anxiety. The American infant does not reach this stage until 10 or 11 months of age."[61] What we should like to know is whether the Ugandan child, because he has so much more of his mother at this early stage in his life, develops a greater sense of inner security than the American child. Both analytical theory and practice would certainly lead one to expect this. It is noteworthy that the Ugandan child also learns to walk sooner than his American counterpart.

At birth the development of the human nervous system is incomplete. The motor tracts are not fully myelinated: that is, they have not acquired the insulating sheaths which are necessary if nervous impulses are to be transmitted properly. Infants, therefore, lack motor co-ordination. It takes a long time for the human infant to become able to stand or walk, and even longer for it to obtain control over bowels and bladder. On the other hand, sensation, the receptive end of the input-output system, is well-developed. Unlike the young of many other species, the newborn human can see, hear and smell. He is also sensitive to pain, touch, and change of position. Touch has been proved by the Harlows to be of great importance in infant monkeys who will cling to a mother surrogate which is soft, warm and furry, in preference to a mother surrogate which is hard, even though the latter is a source of food whilst the former is not. Our use of words demonstrates the importance of haptic sensations, for we speak of being 'in touch with' or 'making contact with' our fellows, even when we are making statements which are psychological and symbolic rather than literal. It is quite possible that the infant's conception of the reality of the external world originally depends principally upon touch (with of course the addition of sight, smell and hearing). Certainly, those children and adults who 'lose touch' with reality and their fellow beings appear to be those who have not, in infant life, developed a close enough contact with the mother for long enough to be sure of her reality as a loving person.

Sherrington once described the human nervous system as a funnel of which the receptive sensory end was the wide end, whilst the effector motor end was the narrow end. Human infants appear to be creatures who are sensitive to and need sensory stimulation, but in whom the motor apparatus is not sufficiently developed for much co-ordinated self-expression. One example of this is the development of speech. The comprehension of words long antedates their use. Babies under six months living in orphanages babble less than those reared in normal homes. There is a good deal of evidence derived from the direct observation of infants which shows that even functions normally under the control of the autonomic system, like breathing and digestion, are easily disorganized; and that their smooth operation depends upon being held and fondled by the mother. Margaret Ribble, in an intensive study of 600 infants, found that "a generalized state of observable muscular tension existed and readily became exaggerated in about 30 per cent of the 600 newborn babies in my study. This tension disappeared when the child sucked or when it was put in close contact with the body of the mother." Babies who were seldom held by their mothers tended to develop gastro-intestinal disorders and showed irregular and shallow respiration.

Very deprived infants show one of two general types

of reaction. The first is described as negativism, and consists of a refusal to suck, combined with loss of appetite and failure to assimilate food. In addition, the infants show rigidity of the body musculature, especially of the muscles of the neck and back, periods of violent screaming, vomiting, breath-holding, shallow breathing and constipation.

The other type of reaction, called regression, is characterized by "a form of depression and regressive quiescence". Such infants make feeble attempts to suck, but then fall into a stuporose sleep from which it is hard to arouse them. There is a general loss of muscle tone, and reflex excitability, which may be so extreme as to resemble the clinical picture of shock. Ribble concludes: "The transition from the vegetative life of the foetus to the independent and reactive life of the infant requires a longer time in man than it does in other mammals, and consistent mothering is required if the human infant is to pass this transition unscarred."[62]

It appears from many researches that adequate mothering is absolutely necessary if the physiological integration of the infant's functioning is to be preserved, and that disorganization of physiological function takes place in the absence of sufficient close and frequent contact with the mother. We know from the study of schizoid and schizophrenic patients that they lack what Laing describes as 'primary ontological security".[63] Such people fear disintegration and disorganization of the very core of their being and many of their peculiarities of behaviour are designed to protect the inner self which "to them, is in perpetual danger

94

of engulfment or destruction". These people are 'out of touch with' their own bodies, which they often feel to be alien from their 'true self'.

Schizoid personalities and schizophrenics fear both the destructive effect of the external world upon them and also their own destructive effect upon the world. It is for this reason that emotional involvement is so difficult for them, for the love which they require and which might, in fact, have an integrating effect upon them, appears to them as a potentially destructive agent. This peculiar state of affairs can, I believe, be understood in terms of the primitive negativistic reaction of the under-mothered infant described by Margaret Ribble.

If an infant is deprived in this way it is clear from observation that it is reacting with what, in an adult, would be called hostility. Harlow's rhesus monkeys who had been early and long isolated reacted with hostility to anyone who approached them, biting, scratching and snarling. Human infants, because of the immaturity of the motor nervous system, cannot co-ordinate a rage response in an effective way until much later in their development. At an earlier point in this essay, I quoted from a Kleinian analyst, Joan Riviere[24] who assumes, like Mrs Klein herself and all her followers, that infants experience 'overwhelming anxiety' as a response to hunger or other frustrations, and that thrashing and crying, responses which are certainly present from birth, are aggressive discharges. Not all observers would agree with this. Konrad Lorenz, the founder of modern ethology, writes: "The only thing which gives me a very small twinge every time I read it, is the Melanie Klein assumption of a great amount of spontaneous aggressivity in the small baby. I know so many animals which are completely unaggressive as nestlings. Mammal as well as bird babies creep over each other and tread on each other without ever showing the slightest sign of being angry, even if the sibling is sitting right on their nose, walking on their face or scratching their eyes. All they can do is give a distress signal which can be shown, by later motivational analysis, to be entirely independent of aggression. Equally independent of aggression is the tremendously strong and voracious motivation of feeding, and all this is true of beasts like ravens, cats, canaries, etc. which are *highly* aggressive in later life. I do believe that in the human baby real aggression matures quite early, long before the child can do anything about it except yelling, but I do feel that I can tell the difference between a pure distress crying, analogous to the distress signal of a gosling and a puppy, and that kind of crying which contains an admixture of rage. I don't deny that this may be detected by a good observer at the age of 2 or 3 months, my point is only that mere feeding and the expression of hunger has little to do with cannibalism and aggression against Ma. This postponing of the maturation phase of aggressivity *would not by any means negate the consequences of the Kleinian theory.*"[64]

Another ethologist, who is an expert on primates, would agree that distress crying and aggression are separate phenomena. "As the months pass, a new pattern of infant behaviour begins to emerge: aggression arrives on the scene. Temper tantrums and angry crying begin to differentiate themselves from the earlier all-purpose crying response. The baby signals its aggression by a more broken, irregular form of screaming and by violent striking out with its arms and legs. It attacks small objects, shakes large ones, spits and spews, and tries to bite, scratch or strike anything in reach. At first these activities are rather random and unco-ordinated. The crying indicates that fear is still present. The aggression has not yet matured to the point of a pure attack: this will come much later when the infant is sure of itself and fully aware of its physical capacities."[65]

There has been a good deal of research which tends to show that babies reared in institutions where the opportunities for inter action with adults are small suffer as a result, however well their needs for food, warmth, and cleanliness are attended to. Such infants show little interest in the environment, are late in attempting to talk, and merely cry in a forlorn and miserable way when frustrated without making any attempt to get what they want from adults. Rage implies some feeling that the object might be induced to behave differently; but if rage is habitually met with no response, or there is no one present to receive the baby's anger, he soon learns to suppress or repress it, and simply turns away. These babies are suffering from a type of depression first described by René Spitz.[66]

In studying adult depression we have become accustomed to the fact that repressed aggression and depression are intimately connected. The depressed person, in heaping abuse upon himself, is deflecting resentment away from someone close to him who seems to him to be rejecting or depriving, and turning it inwards. But are we justified in assuming, as analysts habitually do, that this process of repressing aggression takes place in infants as it does in adults? As Lorenz suggests, we may be failing to distinguish between distress crying and angry crying in infants, and thus attributing to them more aggression than they are capable of. Deprived, institutionalized babies show apathy and withdrawal rather than rage. Is there any evidence that they are storing up resentment which may be 'taken out' at a later date upon those that care for them? The researches of Goldfarb suggest that this may be so. He compared orphans who had been brought up in an institution for the first three years of their lives and then transferred to foster homes, with orphans who had been brought up in foster homes from infancy onwards. He made these comparisons at different ages, ranging from $3\frac{1}{2}$ to 12. The institution-reared children were not only inferior in intelligence tests of all kinds, but also showed much more aggressive behaviour. That is, they told more lies, had more temper tantrums, attacked other children more frequently, and were more destructive of property. This research strongly suggests that the psychoanalysts are right in supposing that the very early environment of the child is all-important. It also, and more depressingly, suggests that, if the early environment is unfavourable enough, the results may be as irreversible as Harlow found with his most severely isolated rhesus monkeys. "Many of the institution-reared were subsequently adopted into foster homes that were intellectually and emotionally more stimulating than the institution. Despite this, they continued to be retarded in mental growth."[67]

Since we cannot enter direct into the emotional experience of the infant, we can only make guesses as to what it may be feeling. But if the infant's thrashing and crying produce no response, or only a very delayed one, it seems likely that this earliest expression of rage is felt as impotent rage rather than as an effective aggressive action. When adults are very frustrated, they show rather similar responses, of which tearing the hair and biting the carpet are two examples. These are essentially displacement activities, and are felt to be ineffective by the person performing them, who often feels even more humiliated and impotent by having given way to a childish display.

Moreover, because of the relative immaturity of the nervous system, it seems probable that emotional situations arise in infancy with which the infant is in no position to deal because it is not physically mature enough to do so. Human infants are subject to stimuli to which they *cannot* provide an adequate response. A parallel in adult life would be that of a person who is tied down and subjected to torture. In such a situation, neither flight nor fight—the two obvious responses to pain—are possible. The result is impotent rage; the rage of the entirely helpless. Jonathan Swift, an example of a man whose inner rage can seldom have been more creatively employed, is surely recalling something of this feeling when he writes of Gulliver visiting the land of giants, Brobdingnag: "That which gave me most Uneasiness among those Maids of Honour, when my Nurse carried me to visit them, was to see them use me without any Manner of Ceremony like a Creature who had no Sort of Consequence."[68]

A study of the methods of interrogation used by the Communist police reveals that it is not too difficult to reduce most human beings to a state closely resembling that of the infants reared in institutions described above. A man arrested by the Soviet State police is first placed in solitary confinement. "A major aspect of his prison experience is isolation. Man is a social animal; he does not live alone. From birth to death he lives in the company of his fellow-men. When he is totally isolated, he is removed from all of the interpersonal relations which are so important to him, and taken out of the social role which sustains him. His internal as well as his external life is disrupted." No one speaks to him; no one answers his questions. Nothing he does has the slightest effect upon his captors, except that infringements of the prison routine may bring punishment. "The period of anxiety, hyperactivity, and apparent adjustment to the isolation routine usually continues from one to three weeks. As it continues the prisoner becomes increasingly dejected and dependent. He gradually gives up all spontaneous activity within his cell and ceases to care about his personal appearance and actions. Finally, he sits and stares with a vacant expression, perhaps endlessly twisting a button on his coat. He allows himself to become dirty and dishevelled. When food is presented to him, he eats it all, but he no longer bothers with the niceties of eating. He may mix it into a mush and stuff it into his mouth like an animal. He goes through the motions of his prison routine automatically, as if he were in a daze. The slop jar is no longer offensive to him. Ultimately he seems to lose many of the restraints of ordinary behavior. He may soil himself. He weeps, he mutters, and he prays aloud in his cell. He follows the orders of the guard with the docility of a trained animal. It usually takes from four to six weeks to produce this phenomenon in a newly imprisoned man."[69]

The reaction described above is predominantly a depressive one, rather than a paranoid state; but it serves to illustrate how easily, and in how short a time, a normal human being can be thrown into a state of profound regression in which infantile mechanisms and behaviour, long since overlaid, are revived and brought to the surface. Paranoid ideas are equally easy to resuscitate.

Another Communist technique which equally illustrates the persistence of infantile emotional constellations beneath the adult surface is the 'friendly approach' suddenly adopted by the interrogator towards the prisoner when he feels that the latter is on the point of total breakdown. "The prisoner, returned once again to an interrogation session that he expects will be a repetition of torture and vilification, suddenly finds that the entire scene has changed. The interrogation room is brightly lighted. The interrogator is seated behind his desk, relaxed and smiling. Tea and cigarettes are waiting on the table. He is ushered to a comfortable chair." The interrogator professes friendship, asks the prisoner about his family, apologizes for former ill-treatment. "Prisoners find this sudden friendship and release of pressure almost irresistible. Nearly all of them avidly seize the opportunity to talk about themselves and their feelings, and then go on to talk about their families. Most of them proceed from this almost automatically to giving the information which the interrogator seeks."[69]

So great is the human need for love, and for positive interaction with other humans, that even a torturer, who temporarily alters his demeanour, will be taken for a "good object", in an emotional sense, although the prisoner may know intellectually that he is nothing of the kind. The infant's alternation of feeling towards those who frustrate and gratify him is equally extreme and indeed the prisoner's behaviour is a repetition of those feelings. Another example of the same phenomenon is to be found in children whose parents are, in reality, altogether rejecting and hostile. Such children will often defend their parents and cling to them, since they have developed no intimate attachments to anyone else, and any parent is, in their eyes, better than none.

The study of psychosis, both naturally occurring, and artificially produced as in the case of 'brainwashing' techniques, is valuable in that it reveals the kind of psychopathology which is present at a deep level in all of us, but which seldom comes to the surface except under special circumstances. The mechanisms revealed are predominantly depressive and paranoid.

It is not only neglect and deprivation of human interaction which may have a traumatic effect upon infants. One theory which used to be popular was that physical restraint was an important determinant of infantile rage. Thus Watson, the founder of Behaviourism, writes: "Observation seemed to show that hampering of the infant's movements is the factor which apart from all training brings out the movements characteristic of rage."[70] Geoffrey Gorer, in his book on the Russians, makes out a fairly convincing case that some facets of the Russian character may be related to the highly restrictive swaddling of the infant which was customary in Russia. He believes that such swaddling causes the infant to experience intense rage which it cannot express; that this rage also gives rise to intense guilt; and that it is projected upon the external world (that is, attributed to others), and consequently causes the child to feel intense fear as well. Gorer believes that the characteristic Russian tendency to confess to crime even when there is no evidence of guilt is derived from this infantile guilt; an hypothesis which will seem convincing to many who remember feeling guilty as schoolboys about offences committed by others. He also suggests that the sudden alternation of brutality with kindness common amongst Russians, and exploited by the secret police in interrogation procedures, may be related to the infant's earliest experience of restriction and solitariness whilst swaddled, alternating with freedom and gratification whilst being breast-fed and unrestrained.[71]

Phyllis Greenacre, reviewing the literature, concludes that tight swaddling may temporarily retard both intellectual and motor development, and probably has a tendency to increase sado-masochistic elements in character. But, as she cogently observes, we need to know much more detail than we can usually obtain about how the swaddling was applied, by whom and with what intensity, before we can make any generally valid statement about the effect of early physical restriction. It is well-recognized, for example, that moderate restraint may quieten a disturbed infant.[72] Indeed, we are not yet in a position to be dogmatic about what are the most traumatic experiences of infancy and early childhood, although we can say with certainty that infantile experience is an important determinant of adult character. As one psychoanalyst wrote recently: "The problem of deciding which are in fact the traumatic experiences of childhood has proved so difficult that it would be possible to write the history of psychoanalysis in terms of various kinds of shocking or frightening experience which have been cast for the role of prime traumatic agent.[73]

The elucidation of what really goes on between an infant and its mother is a difficult task which is still itself in its infancy. We are rightly reluctant to institute controlled studies in which normal infants are subjected to deprivation and discomfort, and compared with normal controls: and even if we had much more of such evidence, it is questionable how much this would really increase our knowledge. We know that neglect, rejection and ill-treatment may cause a child to feel more hate than love towards its parents, and to continue to carry this hatred, or a propensity towards hatred, with it into adult life. But subtler attitudes of disregard, and more complicated, less obvious interactions within a network of family relationships may also have their effect. The scapegoat phenomenon, already mentioned in the context of nations, operates also upon a smaller scale. Within the family, it is not infrequent for one child to be labelled 'bad', and to act as scapegoat for all the problems and conflicts of the others. One such child attempted suicide. Upon her recovery her mother, unable to blame the child for her own difficulties any longer, had to be certified insane. Such complex interactions, although of vital importance, are difficult to study experimentally. For the present we must be content with the admittedly unsatisfactory reconstructions of infantile experience which are derived from the psychoanalysis of children and adults. It is impossible to prove the existence of the violent phantasies attributed to the infant by Kleinian analysts, since they belong to a period of life before the infant can express itself in words. But, as Susan Isaacs points out in her paper "The Nature and Function of Phantasy", "Unconscious phantasies are always inferred, not observed as such; the technique of psychoanalysis as a whole is largely based upon inferred knowledge."[74] Moreover, as Joan Riviere states: "Conclusions about impulses and conflicts arising at a date at which the child has almost no means of *direct* expression must be based on the evidence of repetition in analysis—it is the only source of knowledge of the unconscious mental content existing before consciousness and memory develops fully."[75]

The analytical study of adults reveals that there are a large number of persons who entertain phantasies which suggest that, as infants, they were recurrently subjected to situations in which they felt helplessly under the power of adults who were hostile and recurrently harmful to them. Even if they do not consciously remember such situations, it is by no means absurd to suggest that traces of experiences which were interpreted in this way are imprinted in the nervous system. Man, in any case, is distinguished by the fact that he has an extraordinarily well-developed memory. It is quite possible that some early conditioning takes place before the nervous system is sufficiently developed for all the connections between the cortex and lower centres have become established. Thus some experiences may occur, and may leave their permanent effect and imprint on the brain, which actually *cannot* be remembered.

George Crile in *A Naturalistic View of Man* suggests that childhood amnesia is related to the lag in development of the temporal cortex. "It is probable that in mankind, the crucial period which corresponds to imprinting in the lower creatures encompasses the time of childhood amnesia."

"The experiences of early childhood are firmly recorded in the lower centres of the *old* brain and exert a profound effect on subsequent behavior. However, they are isolated and inviolable. There is no way for them to become connected with the interpretive (temporal) cortex which has not yet developed, and hence they can never be either retrieved as memories or altered by comparison with subsequent experiences. They are like the patterns of behavior that are inherited as instincts, or are acquired as a result of imprintation."[76]

This very interesting suggestion may throw light on some tragically disturbed patients who seem unable to recall the traumata of their early childhood, and who yet, in the analytical situation, give unmistakable evidence of having suffered such traumata, in that they are unable to react to the analyst in any positive way, but continue to regard him as a persecutor.

A less extreme example of a similar reaction is the fear of the dentist which so many 'normal' people experience. People who fear visits to the dentist are not in general exhibiting anxiety which is appropriate to the moderate degree of pain which they may expect to face at the hands of a modern, humane dental surgeon. They are filled with a dread which would only be appropriate if they were going to be tied down and interrogated by secret police. Most people who are phobic about the dentist never conceive of the situation as one in which they have the power to walk out, or even to retaliate upon the dentist if his ministrations become painful. They imagine themselves as powerless; the dentist as omnipotent; and they envisage him, not as a healer whom they are employing, but as a potential torturer.

I suggest that, because of the extreme immaturity and dependence of the human infant at birth, *all* human beings know, at some deep level of their being, what it is to feel utterly helpless. I suggest also, in line with the findings of Kleinian analysts, that a sharp division between 'good' and 'bad' takes place very early in infantile experience, according to the infant's alternating experience of satisfaction and frustration. Therefore, all human infants have some experience of feeling both helpless and frustrated, and, at the same time, in the hands of powerful figures who appear 'evil', however 'good' and predominantly benign their actual parents may have been.

These considerations, I believe, go some way toward explaining why so many normal human beings will behave cruelly to members of their own kind, if given the chance, or if encouraged by authority to do so. For enemies, whatever their real character, easily become the carriers of paranoid projections, and are thus transformed from being merely human opponents into malignant, powerful persecutors. To have such an enemy in one's power is to give many human beings an opportunity for revenge upon which they act with alacrity. No torment is too extreme for those who have tormented one; no humiliation is too great for those who have exploited one's own impotent helplessness. The pleasure which men obtain from tormenting the helpless victim is understandable, though no less distasteful, when we take into account the element of revenge. Cruelty is more closely linked with the pleasure of power than with the pleasure of sex; and those to whom it has the most appeal are those who have most felt themselves to be insulted and injured.

Since all human infants are bound to have experienced some frustrations and feelings of helplessness, it follows that all human beings carry with them into adult life some degree of resentment, however small. But, how human beings deal with their proclivity to hatred and destructiveness varies in accordance with many factors, including both the way they are reared, and also the social milieu in which they find themselves. Broadly speaking, there are two main methods which human beings employ to deal with internal rage, the paranoid and the depressive. In extreme form, either method is 'pathological'; but traces of both paranoid and depressive mechanisms are detectable in normal human beings. Indeed, I share the conceptions of W. R. D. Fairbairn in considering that the neurotic defences with which we are so familiar in clinical practice, including hysterical, obsessional and phobic techniques, are devices protecting the individual from relapsing into depressive despair or a schizoid sense of utter futility.

The paranoid technique for dealing with internal rage is to project it upon persons in the environment. "It is not I who is violent and destructive, but they." This preserves self-esteem, but makes the environment and the people in it threatening and 'bad'. The depressive technique achieves just the opposite. The depressive deals with anger by turning it against himself in self-reproach and self-destructiveness. This manoeuvre preserves the environment as 'good' and therefore protective, but is at the expense of the individual's own self-esteem.

A very simple example of the use of these techniques is the differing manner in which students react in face of failure in an examination. One will blame the examiners, whom he concludes to have been prejudiced, unfair or careless; thus attributing the 'bad' to the environment, whilst preserving himself as 'good'. The other will blame himself, and abuse himself for being lazy, stupid, and feckless; thus preserving the environment as 'good' at the expense of labelling himself as 'bad'.

Carried to extremes, the paranoid attitude leads to murder; whilst the depressive attitude leads to suicide. That both mechanisms can be operative within the same individual (though not at exactly the same moment) is demonstrated by the fact that one in three murderers commit suicide. Indeed, D. J. West, in his study *Murder followed by Suicide* writes: "Sometimes the aggressive urge is divided so evenly between homicidal and suicidal impulses that some quite trifling circumstance may have sufficient weight to tip the scales one way or the other." He goes on to refer to "the hair's breadth division between murder and suicide in many a rejected lover".[77]

This relation between homicide and suicide is borne out by various studies of the murder rates compared with the suicide rates in the Southern states of America. "Austin Porterfield, in 1949, using mortality tables from 'Vital Statistics' brought the murder and suicide indices together and showed that there was a general inverse relationship between the two rates among the states, and the Southern states ranked highest in homicide and lowest in suicide." What determines whether a country or state has a relatively high suicide rate compared with the murder rate, or *vice versa*? The author concludes that: "Though the data are extremely questionable, there is a significant positive correlation between the suicide-homicide ratio for the 56 world polities for which information is readily available and almost every measure of modernization which can be quantified."[78] Of these measures of modernization, education appears to be the most important.

In other words, the suicide rate rises, and the homicide rate diminishes, as the level of education in a community rises. We have long suspected, as Dr Winnicott once said, that Western civilization is predominantly a "depressive" culture. Psychiatrists working in Nigeria have noted that, in primitive villages, the most common form of psychotic breakdown is an acute paranoid state, in which the individual goes berserk, believes that he is persecuted or bewitched, and often attacks his ostensible persecutors. The depressed form of psychotic reaction, so common in our culture, in which the individual torments himself with self-reproach, and often commits suicide, is practically unknown. As the villagers become progressively Westernized, the neuroses and depressive states so familiar to us become more common, and the paranoid reactions less so.

Moreover, there are investigations which suggest that the way a child is brought up within the family may determine whether he uses predominantly depressive or paranoid mechanisms for dealing with his aggression. In a comparative study of depressed and paranoid patients, it was found that: "Depressed patients came from families in which the children were forced to try by themselves to attain the desired forms of behavior through positive 'ought' channels. Children in the families of paranoid patients were forced into acceptable modes of behavior by negative 'ought not' procedures.

"In families of *depressed* patients the child comes to view his environment as non-threatening to him physically. It is something to be manipulated by him in order to bring about the desired effects that will win approval. There is directionality here, and it is *from* the child *toward* his environment. On the other hand, in families of *paranoid* patients the child comes to view his environment as having potentially harmful properties that he cannot control and that must be avoided in some way. Here the directionality is *from* the environment *toward* the child."[79]

In other words, although overcrowding, urbaniza-
tion, the presence of alien minorities, and many other
social factors of great importance contribute their
share to violence in society, there is increasing evidence
that the way children are reared, both in infancy and
later childhood, is a potent factor in determining how
they will handle their aggression. To some extent, it
appears that we can choose whether children will learn
the paranoid technique or the depressive.

But need they learn either? Is it possible, or indeed
desirable, that we should raise our children in such a
way that they have no propensity to react aggressively?
Elsewhere, I have given my reasons for supposing that
the aggressive drive in human beings is not merely the
product of frustration, infantile or otherwise. I have
also alleged that it has many positive functions, and
that it is only when the aggressive drive is itself obstructed that frustration may drive the individual into
hatred and violence. This is not the place to repeat
those arguments; nor is it my function to suggest that
human violence and destructiveness can be abolished
or substantially modified by Utopian social measures
which could be immediately adopted.

Nevertheless, it does seem possible that we could
avoid producing some of the more destructive individuals in our society if we knew more about the best
ways of rearing infants.

At least some anthropologists believe that this is so.
One such anthropologist is Richard de Boer, who has
made a special study of the Eskimos of the Central
Canadian Arctic. According to his observation, Eskimo
mothers practise what he calls 'extero-gestation'. That

is, from the time of birth until the infant is independently mobile, the mother endeavours to see that its environment differs as little as possible from the environment of the womb. "In these societies, infants are carried about constantly, slept with at night, and the sensory route of communication is tactile which facilitates a response to infant stimuli (e.g. sucking and rooting reflex) that precludes crying behavior and restricts frustration to about the same level the infant enjoyed in utero where homeostasis is maintained biochemically through the mediatory functions of the placenta. In a sense, the tactile perceptor extra-utero is analogous to the placenta and, in fact, the entire process of extero-gestation is an analog of intero-gestation. In the Netsilik Eskimo society, extero-gestation is functional *in toto* until the acquisition of locomotor ability and persists where required until cognition." Mr de Boer disputes my belief that a certain amount of infant frustration is inevitable. "In the Eskimo culture, it is considered grossly abnormal for infants to cry. For Eskimo mothers, crying is not a signal, but more accurately a sign indicating a grossly abnormal state of infant hypertension and stress."

The result of this kind of infant rearing is that "aggressive behavior cannot be elicited from an Eskimo," that there is no dominance hierarchy, and that the "Eskimo culture is one of the few societies recorded in the ethnographic literature that has never gone to war". "The Eskimo has practised the precepts of Karl Marx for over five thousand years and during which time they maintained an unusually viable and stable culture

without resorting to any kind of dominance hierarchy." "Eskimos do not defend or have conflicts over
territory. Eskimos are not possessive, in fact just the
opposite, they share everything, food, wives, husbands,
children, tools and shelter."

Sceptical, I pressed Mr de Boer to modify his statement about aggressive behaviour and he did go so far
as to admit that "there are certainly pathological individuals among the Eskimos and they are recognized
for being just that. . . . Occasionally a situation will
arise where there are two or more asocial individuals
living in the same community and oddly enough ani-
mosity is usually reciprocal between these individuals
rather than being vented hither and thither on various
individuals among the community at large. These individuals will usually make defamatory remarks about
one another and if the tension created is of sufficient
magnitude they will challenge each other to a drum
duel where each will dance and chant derisive remarks
in song directed at the other. Historically speaking,
this is often the end of ill feelings, at least in many of
the recorded cases, and reconciliation is effected."

Still sceptical, I suggested that Mr de Boer was
idealizing his Eskimos, a fault to which anthropologists
are sometimes prone. He was very willing to consider
that this might be a possibility. I also asked him, since
he clearly considers the culture of Western Europe and
the U.S.A. to be seriously pathological, whether there
were any other peoples in the world besides the
Eskimos whom he considered were *not* pathological.
His answer was as follows: "Not quite. The pre-World
War II Okinawans, the Lepchas, the Dyaks of Borneo,

and the mountain Arapesh are apparently very normal in their interpersonal relationships, but most of these groups put an emphasis on the group to the exclusion of the individual. There should be no dichotomy between the interests of the group and the interests of the individual, each should complement the other.''[80] The cultures he lists do not, it will be perceived, constitute a high proportion of mankind. But the value of Mr de Boer's research, even if he is overstating his case, is that, once again, it draws attention to the possibility of modifying man's cruelty and destructiveness by paying attention to infant rearing.

We shall have to live with the fact of man's paranoid potential so far as the foreseeable future is concerned; and this means that we shall also have to live with human cruelty and destructiveness. Gradually, we shall hope to learn more of the social and political forces which activate this paranoid potential, and which result in the horrors of violence and cruelty which we are concerned to abolish. But social and political forces originate with the individual. In their concern with 'larger issues' it is to be hoped that our leaders will not forget that research into the relation of adult behaviour with methods of infant rearing deserves the fullest possible support. There is no short answer to the problem of human destructiveness. Let us hope that a longer look at the way the human animal develops may eventually produce some modification in our violent and destructive species.

# References

1. FRANK, Jerome D. *Sanity and Survival* (London: Barrie & Rockliff, The Cresset Press, 1968; New York: Random House, 1968).

2. BURTON, John. 'The Nature of Aggression as revealed in the Atomic Age' in *The Natural History of Aggression*, ed. Carthy and Ebling (London: Academic Press, 1964), p. 150.

3. BRØNSTED, Johannes. *The Vikings* (Harmondsworth: Penguin Books, 1960), p. 26.

4. MONTAGU, M. F. Ashley (ed.). *Man and Aggression* (New York and London: Oxford University Press, 1968), pp. xii, 11, 16.

5. WASHBURN, S. L. 'Conflict in Primate Society' in *Conflict in Society*, ed. de Reuck and Knight (London: J. & A. Churchill, 1966), p. 11.

6. BIGELOW, Robert. *The Dawn Warriors* (Boston: Atlantic Monthly, 1969; London: Hutchinson, 1970), p. 200.

7. LORENZ, Konrad. *Studies in Animal and Human Behaviour* Vol. 1 (London: Methuen & Co, 1970; Cambridge, Mass.: Harvard University Press, 1970), p. xiii.

8. RYCROFT, Charles. *A Critical Dictionary of Psychoanalysis* (London: Nelson, 1968; New York: Basic Books, 1969), p. 5.

9. SCHILDER, Paul. 'Action, Impulsion, Aggression' in *Contributions to Developmental Neuro-Psychiatry* (London: Tavistock, 1964; New York: International Universities Press, 1964), pp. 283, 242-3.

10. SCHILDER, Paul. 'Personality Development' in *Contributions to Developmental Neuro-Psychiatry*, p. 64.

# REFERENCES

11. ONIANS, R. B. *The Origins of European Thought* (Cambridge: University Press, 1954), p. 21.

12. RYCROFT, Charles. 'Introduction: Causes and Meaning' in *Psychoanalysis Observed*, ed. Rycroft (London: Constable, 1966; New York: Coward McCann, 1967), p. 21.

13. WYNNE-EDWARDS, V. C. *Animal Dispersion in Relation to Social Behaviour* (Edinburgh: Oliver and Boyd, 1962; New York: Hafner, 1962), pp. 12, 14.

14. SCHULTZ, Adolph H. *The Life of Primates* (London: Weidenfeld & Nicolson, 1969; New York: Universe Books, 1969), pp. 239-40.

15. COON, Carleton S. *The Living Races of Man* (New York: Knopf, 1965; London: Jonathan Cape, 1966), pp. 14, 3.

16. ZUCKERMAN, S. *The Social Life of Monkeys and Apes* (London: Kegan Paul, Trench, Trubner, 1932).

17. RUSSELL, Claire and RUSSELL, W. M. S. *Violence, Monkeys and Man* (London: Macmillan, 1968), p. 3.

18. MILGRAM, S. 'Behavioral Study of Obedience', *J. Abn. and Soc. Psychology*, 67 (1963), pp. 371-8.

19. MILGRAM, S. 'Some Conditions of Obedience and Disobedience to Authority', *Human Relations*, *18* (1965), pp. 57-76.

20. CHANCE, Michael R. A. and JOLLY, Clifford J. *Social Groups of Monkeys, Apes and Men*, Chapter III (London: Jonathan Cape, 1970; New York: Dutton, 1970), pp. 48-113.

21. BERKOWITZ, Leonard. *Aggression. A Social Psychological Analysis* (New York: McGraw-Hill, 1962), p. 291.

22. PARKER, Tony. *The Frying-Pan* (London: Hutchinson, 1970; New York: Basic Books, 1970), p. 86.

23. EYSENCK, H. J. *Crime and Personality* (London: Routledge & Kegan Paul, 1964), p. 62.

24. RIVIERE, Joan. 'Psychical Conflict in Earliest Infancy' in *Developments in Psychoanalysis* (London: Hogarth Press and Institute of Psycho-Analysis, 1952; New York: Hillary House), p. 44.

25. MARCUS, Steven. *The Other Victorians* (London: Weidenfeld & Nicolson, 1966; New York: Basic Books, 1966), p. 263.

26. KINSEY, Alfred C. *et al.* *Sexual Behavior in the Human Female* (Philadelphia and London: Saunders, 1953), pp. 677, 687.

27. BROWN, Roger. *Social Psychology* (New York: The Free Press, 1965; London: Collier-Macmillan), p. 74.

28. MASLOW, A. H. *et al.* Some Parallels between Sexual and Dominance Behavior of Infra-Human Primates and the Fantasies of Patients in Psychotherapy.' *Journal of Nervous and Mental Disease, 131* (1960), pp. 202-12.

29. CHANCE, Michael R. A. and JOLLY, Clifford J. *Social Groups of Monkeys, Apes and Men*, p. 187.

30. WICKLER, Wolfgang. 'Socio-sexual Signals and their Intraspecific Imitation among Primates' in *Primate Ethology*, ed. by Desmond Morris (London: Weidenfeld & Nicolson, 1967).

31. FREUD, Sigmund. *The Interpretation of Dreams*, trans. by James Strachey. *The Standard Edition of the Complete Psychological Works of Sigmund Freud*, Vol. V (London: Hogarth Press), p. 354.

32. MOHR, J. W., TURNER, R. E. and JERRY, M. B. *Pedophilia and Exhibitionism* (Canada: University of Toronto Press, 1964).

33. SPITZ, H. H. A. 'Clinical Investigation of Certain Personality Characteristics of Twenty Male Exhibitionists.' *Disserta Abstr., 16* (1956), pp. 381-92.

34. FENICHEL, Otto. *The Psychoanalytic Theory of Neurosis* (New York: Norton, 1945; London: Routledge & Kegan Paul, 1946), p. 358.

35. FREUD, Sigmund. *Three Essays on the Theory of Sexuality* trans. by James Strachey. *Standard Edition*, Vol. VII, pp. 157-8.

36. *Ibid.* p. 159.

37. FREUD, Sigmund. 'The Sexual Life of Human Beings' in *Introductory Lectures on Psychoanalysis*, trans. by James Strachey. *Standard Edition*, Vol. XVI, p. 306.

38. FREUD, Sigmund. 'The Economic Problem of Masochism.' *Standard Edition*, Vol. XIX, p. 163.

39. MARCUS, Steven. *The Other Victorians*, p. 194.

40. REAGE, Pauline. *Histoire d'O* (Paris: Jean-Jacques Pauvert, 1962).

41. FENICHEL, Otto. *The Psychoanalytic Theory of Neurosis*, p. 40.

42. DEUTSCH, Helene. *The Psychology of Women* (New York: Grune & Stratton, 1945; London: Research Books, 1947), p. 201.

43. HORNEY, Karen. *Feminine Psychology* (London: Routledge & Kegan Paul, 1967; New York: Norton, 1967), p. 232.

44. FENICHEL, Otto. *The Psychoanalytic Theory of Neurosis*, p. 231.

45. KOBBE, Gustav. *The Complete Opera Book* (London: Putnam, 1953), p. 920.

46. FREUD, Sigmund. 'Femininity' in *New Introductory Lectures on Psychoanalysis. Standard Edition*, Vol. XXII, p. 125.

47. HORNEY, Karen. 'On the Genesis of the Castration Complex in Women' in *Feminine Psychology*, p. 38.

48. TIGER, Lionel. *Men in Groups* (London: Nelson, 1969; New York: Random House, 1969), p. 73.

49. RYCROFT, Charles. *Anxiety and Neurosis* (London: Allen Lane The Penguin Press, 1968; Baltimore: Penguin, 1970), p. 92.

50. De BEAUVOIR, Simone. *The Marquis de Sade* (London: Calder, 1962), pp. 33, 46.

51. KINSEY, Alfred C. *et al. Sexual Behavior in the Human Female*, p. 705.

52. WASHBURN, S. L. 'Role of Conflict in Human Evolution' (discussion) in *Conflict in Society*, p. 57.

53. KRAMER, Heinrich and SPRENGER, James. *Malleus Maleficarum*, trans. Montague Summers (London: Hogarth Press), p. 47 *et seq.*

54. COHN, Norman. *Warrant for Genocide* (London: Eyre and Spottiswoode, 1967; New York: Harper & Row, 1967), p. 153.

55. KOESTLER, Arthur. *The Ghost in the Machine* (London: Hutchinson, 1967; New York: Macmillan, 1968).

56. HUXLEY, Julian. *The Uniqueness of Man* (London: Chatto & Windus, 1941), p. 13.

57. HARLOW, Harry F. 'The Primate Socialization Motive' in *Social Psychiatry*, Vol. I, ed. Ari Kiev (London: Routledge & Kegan Paul, 1970), p. 415.

58. CHANCE, Michael R. A. and JOLLY, Clifford J. *Social Groups of Monkeys, Apes and Men*, Chapter IV, pp. 114-41.

59. HARLOW, Harry F. 'The Primate Socialization Motive' in *Social Psychiatry*, Vol. I, ed. Ari Kiev, p. 404.

60. AINSWORTH, M. D. S. *Infancy in Uganda* (Baltimore and London: Johns Hopkins Press, 1967).

# REFERENCES

61. MUSSEN, Paul H., CONGER, John J. and KAGAN, Jerome. *Child Development and Personality*, 3rd edition (London and New York: Harper & Row, 1969), p. 226.

62. RIBBLE, Margaret A. 'Infantile Experience in Relation to Personality Development' in *Personality and the Behaviour Disorders*, Vol. II, ed. J. McV. Hunt (New York: The Ronald Press, 1944), pp. 629, 633, 635.

63. LAING, R. D. *The Divided Self* (London: Tavistock, 1960; New York: Pantheon, 1970).

64. LORENZ, Konrad. Private communication, 1968.

65. MORRIS, Desmond. *The Naked Ape* (London: Jonathan Cape, 1968; New York: Dell, 1969), pp. 123-4.

66. SPITZ, René and WOLF, K. M. 'Anaclitic Depression: an enquiry into the genesis of psychiatric conditions in early childhood' in *The Psychoanalytic Study of the Child*, Vol. II (London: Hogarth Press, 1946), pp. 313-42.

67. MUSSEN, Paul H., CONGER, John J. and KAGAN, Jerome. *Child Development and Personality*, 3rd edition, p. 234.

68. SWIFT, Jonathan. 'A Voyage to Brobdingnag' in *Gulliver's Travels* and *Selected Writing in Prose and Verse*, ed. J. HAYWARD (London: Nonesuch Press, 1963), p. 115.

69. HINKLE, Lawrence, E. and WOLF, Harold G. 'Communist Interrogation and Indoctrination of "Enemies of the States",' *Arch. Neurol. and Psychiat.*, 1956, pp. 115-74.

70. WATSON, J. B. *Psychology from the Standpoint of the Behaviorist* (Philadelphia: Lippincott, 1919), p. 200.

71. GORER, Geoffrey. *The People of Great Russia* (London: The Cresset Press, 1949; New York: Norton, 1962), p. 122 *et seq.*

72. GREENACRE, Phyllis. *Trauma, Growth and Personality* (London: Hogarth Press, 1953; New York: International Universities Press, 1969), pp. 7, 8.

73. RYCROFT, Charles. *Anxiety and Neurosis*, p. 29.

74. ISAACS, Susan. 'The Nature and Function of Phantasy' in *Developments in Psychoanalysis*, ed. Joan Riviere, p. 69.

75. RIVIERE, Joan. 'Psychical Conflict in Earliest Infancy' in *Developments in Psychoanalysis*, p. 39.

76. CRILE, George. *A Naturalistic View of Man* (New York: World Publishing Co., 1969), pp. 27, 31.

77. WEST, D. J. *Murder followed by Suicide* (London: Heinemann, 1965; Cambridge, Mass.: Harvard University Press, 1965), pp. 114-15.

78. GRAHAM, H. D. and GURR, T. R. *Violence in America* (New York: Bantam Books, 1969), pp. 506, 512.

79. GRAHAM, H. D. and GURR, T. R. *Violence in America*, pp. 522-3, quoting HITSON, H. M. and FUNKENSTEIN, D. H. 'Family Patterns and Paranoidal Personality Structure in Boston and Burma' in *International Journal of Social Psychiatry*, Vol. V, Winter 1959.

80. De BOER, Richard J. Private communication, 1968.

# INDEX

Aggression
definition of, 15-17
handling of, 32, 111-12
in infants, 95-9
in young animals, 96
nature of human, 9-33
repressed, and depression, 18, 97-8
sex differences in, 51, 68, 69-70
sexuality and, 51, 56, 57, 60, 69
Ainsworth, M. D. S., 121
Amnesia
childhood, 106
hysterical, 34
Anti-Semitism, 83-4
*Anxiety and Neurosis*, 71
Apocrine glands, 26
Ardrey, Robert, 13
Authority
obedience to, 29-31, 52

Behaviourism, 102
Behaviour therapy, 41
Berkowitz, Leonard, 37
Bigelow, Robert, 14
Brady, Ian, 48, 72
Brainwashing, 102
Brønsted, Johannes, 11
Brown, Roger, 52
Burton, John, 10

Castration threat, 59
Chance, Michael R. A., 90
Childhood
amnesia, 106

development of conscience in, 37-8, 42, 44
effects of unhappy, 28, 44, 76-7
emotional needs in, 38-9, 42, 44, 76, 78, 104
punishment in, 36-7, 44-5, 67
trauma in, 104, 106
Child-rearing
and aggression, 111-12
love-orientated methods of, 38
Cohn, Norman, 83
Competition
conventional, 23-4
for mates, 25, 64
for resources, 21
in females, 71
in insects and rodents, 25-6
Concentration camps, 9, 10, 49, 77
Conditionability
constitutional differences in, 40
Conger, John J., 91
Conscience
development of, 37-8, 42, 44
Conversion symptoms, 34
Coon, Carleton S., 26
Crile, George, 106
*Crime and Personality*, 40
Criminality
twin studies of, 40-1
Cruelty, 27, 31-2, 86
and sexuality, 60, 72, 74-5
early experience and, 44, 77-8
'normal' propensity to, 80
power and, 76, 107-8
violence distinct from, 46

123

Death instinct, 17-18, 20-1, 61
De Beauvoir, Simone, 74
De Boer, Richard J., 112-15
Defence mechanisms
    neurotic, 35, 108-9
Delusional beliefs, 34, 35, 81-6
Depression, 18, 94, 97-8
Depressive position, 87
Depressive reaction, 101, 108-9,
    111
Deutsch, Helene, 65
Display, 24, 56-7
Dominance
    and submission, 53-6, 57, 69
    hierarchies, 30, 52, 64, 69, 113
    theme in pornography, 62, 64
Doyle, Sir Arthur Conan, 49

Economic Problem of Masochism,
    The, 61
English, the, 12-13
Environment
    over-exploitation of, 21-2
Eskimos
    child-rearing methods of, 112-
    115
Exhibitionism, 58-9
Extero-gestation, 112-13
Eysenck, H. J., 40, 41

Fairbairn, W. R. D., 108
Fear
    as factor in aggression, 10,
    11
    of dentist, 107
    of women, 73
Fenichel, Otto, 63
Flagellation, 49
Foetalization, 88
Frank, Jerome D., 10, 29

Freud, Sigmund, 17, 20, 60-1,
    65, 68, 69, 86-7
Frigidity
    hysterical, 66-8
Frustration
    and aggression, 10, 11, 13, 45-6
    in infancy, 47, 95, 102, 107,
    108, 113
Frying-Pan, The, 41
Fulbright, Senator J. William, 10

Gilbert, W. S., 49
Goldfarb, W., 98
Gorer, Geoffrey, 103
Graham, H. D., 122
'Grasp' reflex, 90
Greenacre, Phyllis, 103
Gurr, T. R., 122

Harkaway, Jack, 48
Harlow, Harry F., 89, 90, 92,
    95, 98
Heath, Neville, 48, 72
Hermes, ithyphallic, 58
Hinkle, Lawrence E., 121
Histoire d'O, 62
Horney, Karen, 65, 68
Hostility, 11, 59, 85
    due to isolation, 95
    group, 14, 26
    parental, to child, 102, 105
    repressed, 32, 37
Huxley, Julian, 88

Immaturity
    prolonged, in man, 23, 69, 88-
    89, 90, 107
Imprinting, 106
Impulse control, 12, 32, 37, 41,
    45, 46, 48

Infancy
depression in, 94, 97
deprivation in, 93-5, 104
emotional expression in, 47, 95-9, 103
mother's role in, 38, 90-4, 104
role in bodily contact and touch in, 90-3
sensori-motor development in, 92-3, 113
swaddling in, 102-4
*See also* Frustration
Infant-rearing, 79
in America and Uganda, 90-2
in Eskimos, 112-13
in institutions, 97-8
Inquisition, 29
*Interpretation of Dreams, The*, 58
Interrogation
Communist methods of, 100-2
Isaacs, Susan, 105
Isolation
as interrogation method, 100-1
experimental, in rhesus monkeys, 89, 95, 98

Jerry, M. B., 118
Jolly, Clifford J., 117, 118, 120
Jung, C. G., 58

Kagan, Jerome, 91
Kinsey, Alfred C., 50, 51, 75
Klein, Melanie, 12, 95, 96
Kleinian theory, 105, 107
Kobbé, Gustav, 119
Koestler, Arthur, 88
Kramer, Heinrich, 81

Laing, R. D., 94
Lange, C. G., 40

*La Nouvelle Justine*, 74
Lawrence, T. E., 36
*Les 120 journées de Sodome*, 74
Literature
sado-masochistic themes in, 48-49
Lorenz, Konrad, 13, 15, 95, 98

*Malleus Maleficarum*, 81-3
Manic patients, 35
Marcus, Steven, 49, 61-2, 63
Marx, Karl, 113
Maslow, Abraham H., 52-3
Masters, John, 57
Mastery
instinct for, 60-1, 69
Memory, 106
*Men in Groups*, 70
Mental retardation, 98, 103
Milgram, S., 29, 77
Mohr, J. W., 118
Montagu, M. F. Ashley, 13-14, 15
Morris, Desmond, 121
Murder, 72, 74
and suicide, 109-10
*Murder followed by Suicide*, 109
Mussen, Paul H., 91

*Naturalistic View of Man, A.*, 106
Neoteny, 88
Nervous system
development of, 89, 92, 105-6
immaturity of human infant's, 95, 99
Neurotics, 34, 35, 73
Nigeria
paranoia in, 110

Onians, R. B., 19
*Other Victorians, The*, 61

Overcrowding, 11, 14, 24, 27, 28, 112

Paedophilia, 63-4
Paranoia
  ubiquity of, 80-115
Paranoid reaction
  *v.* depressive, to internal rage, 108-9, 111
Paranoid-schizoid position, 80, 87
Parker, Tony, 39, 41
Penis envy, 68-9, 70
Phantasies
  incorporation, 63
  infants' violent, 105
  rape, 65
  sado-masochistic, 49
Pornography, 64, 74
  sado-masochistic themes in, 49, 61-3
Porterfield, Austin, 110
Power, power relations, 70, 72
  and cruelty, 76, 107-8
  children and, 65-6, 68, 105
  desire for, in women, 70
  sado-masochism and, 73, 75
  sexual activity in terms of, 59, 66-7
  will to. *See* Mastery, instinct for
Presenting, 53-5
Primitive man, 14-15, 31
Projection, 11, 80, 84, 85, 86, 103, 108, 109
Pseudo-sex, 53, 68, 71, 75-6
Psychoanalysis, 12-13, 65, 105
Psychopaths, aggressive
  absence of parental love in, 38-9, 42, 44, 45, 76

constitutional abnormalities in, 39-40, 45
  conscience in, 37, 42
  lack of impulse control in, 35, 37, 39, 41, 45, 46, 72
  lying in, 43-4
  relationships of, 42-3
  violence of, 36-7, 44, 46
Psychopathy, 34-47, 110-11, 114
  categories of, 34-5
Psychosis, 34, 102
Psychotic depressives, 35
Puccini, G., 67
Punishment
  experimental study of, 29
  of children, 36-7, 44-5, 67

Racial differences, 26
Racial prejudice, 83-6
Réage, Pauline, 119
Reassurance mechanisms, 56, 59, 90
Ribble, Margaret A., 93, 95
Ritual combat, 24-5, 27, 72
Rivière, Joan, 95, 105
Russell, Claire, 27-8, 31, 52-3, 76
Russell, W. M. S., 27-8, 31, 76
Russians, 103
Rycroft, Charles, 16, 71

Sade, Marquis de, 74
Sado-masochism, 48-79
  as pseudo-sex, 71
  increased by swaddling, 103
  male interest in, 50-1
  psychoanalytic view of, 59-61
*Sanity and Survival*, 10, 29
Scapegoat phenomenon, 84, 104
Schilder, Paul, 17
Schizoid personalities, 94-5

Schizophrenics, 34-5, 94-5
Schultz, Adolph H., 117
Separation anxiety, 91
Sexual arousal
    physiology of, and anger, 75
Sexual behaviour
    non-sexual functions of, 53-9
    *See also* Pseudo-sex
*Sexual Behavior in the Human Female*, 75
Sexual offences, 41, 58
Sexual symbolism, 57-8, 68-9, 70
Sherrington, Sir Charles, 93
Smell
    groups distinguished by, 25-6
*Social Life of Monkeys and Apes*, 27
Soviet Union, 24
*Spectator, The*, 84
Speech, 93
Spitz, H. H. A., 118
Spitz, René, 97
Sprenger, James, 81
Stress
    violence due to, 27-9, 31, 76
Suicide, 104, 111
    murder and, 109-10
Summers, Revd. Montague, 82-3
Swift, Jonathan, 99

Territoriality, 22, 57-8, 114
Threat mechanisms, 24, 56-7
*Three Essays on the Theory of Sexuality*, 60

Tiger, Lionel, 70
*Times, The*, 83
Turandot, Princess, 67-8
Turner, R. E., 118

U.S.A., 24

Viking raids, 11-12
Violence
    class differences in, 36
    distinguished from cruelty, 46
    factors predisposing to, 26-9,
        31, 37, 44-6, 76, 112
    in animal communities, 27
    sexuality and, 75
    socially sanctioned, 14, 20

War, 9, 10, 113
    aggression in, 19
    evolutionary effect of, 14
    over-population and, 11, 28
*Warrant for Genocide*, 83
Washburn, S. L., 20, 78
Watson, J. B., 102
West, D. J., 109
Wickler, Wolfgang, 118
Winnicott, D. W., 110
Witchcraft, 81-3
Wolf, Harold G., 121
Wolf, K. M., 121
Wynne-Edwards, V. C., 22, 23, 24

Zuckerman, S., 27

Bradford College Library

BF575.A3 S82                    BCHA